Commonsense Cataloging

Rosalind E. Miller & Jane C. Terwillegar

Commonsense Cataloging

A Cataloger's Manual

Fourth Edition Revised

The H.W. WILSON COMPANY • 1990 • New York

Printed in the United States of America

Library of Congress Cataloging-in-Publication Data

Miller, Rosalind E.
    Commonsense cataloging : a cataloger's manual / Rosalind E. Miller
& Jane C. Terwillegar. — 4th ed. rev.
        p.   cm.
    Includes bibliographical references.
    ISBN 0-8242-0789-0
    1. Cataloging—Handbooks, manuals, etc.   I. Terwillegar, Jane C.
II. Title.
Z693.M54   1990
025.3—dc20   89-70716
                                                              CIP

WHEN THE First Edition of *Commonsense Cataloging* was published in 1965, it was intended to serve as a manual for the beginning cataloger, trained or untrained. The author, Esther Piercy, expressed the hope that the book would "dispel some of the fears, mystery, superstitions, and mystique which sometimes surround the word 'cataloging'" and would enable the librarian to "decide, first, what purposes the collection is intended to serve, and then how best to organize the materials to perform the services." The Fourth Edition Revised has the very same goals. Since 1965, of course, the use by catalogers of computers has greatly increased, but the essential mission of cataloging has remained unchanged. This edition is intended, then, not only for beginning catalogers, but also for all librarians who seek a commonsense approach to cataloging that will help them be more effective amid the changing context of their work.

Throughout the Fourth Edition Revised, the emphasis is on solutions to the practical problems a librarian is likely to encounter, particularly in smaller collections. Special attention is given to the task of adapting prepared catalog copy to local needs. The text, while it reflects the 1988 revision of AACR2, also offers examples of the varied formats of cataloging records facing modern catalogers, many of them prepared from earlier codes and superseded editions. Thus, *Commonsense Cataloging* offers practical advice on such problems as: How much cataloging data should be in a standardized format? When should purchased copy be revised? Should the revised rules in new editions of cataloging tools be adopted immediately? And can complicated nonprint materials or unpublished items be cataloged in a standard, yet simplified format?

As might be expected in such a work, a number of librarians have contributed to this edition. The staff of Pullen Library, Georgia State University, especially Judith Shelton, has been extremely helpful. Others have suggested timely revisions as well, including Thomas E. Sullivan and Stella Lee, both formerly of The H. W. Wilson Company. As always, the authors appreciate the suggestions and comments from their many students.

We also wish to thank Forest Press, Inc., Baker & Taylor Company, and OCLC Online Computer Library Center for their permission to reproduce excerpts from their publications.

Atlanta, Georgia   Rosalind E. Miller
West Palm Beach, Florida   Jane C. Terwillegar
December, 1989

AT HIS DEATH in 1519, Leonardo da Vinci left more than 10,000 sheets of manuscript recording a lifetime's speculation and research in art, mathematics, biology, engineering, and architecture. Of this extraordinary record of genius only some 7,000 sheets are known to have survived, but it is hoped that the remainder were not destroyed and will someday reappear. Hence the excitement when, in 1967, Professor Jules Piccus of the University of Massachusetts discovered two leatherbound volumes containing 700 sheets of Leonardo's notebooks in the National Library of Madrid. The presence of these volumes in the library had long been known: they were recorded in the catalog but had been mis-shelved during the 19th century, and several searches had failed to bring them to light. Professor Piccus, looking for medieval ballads, had stumbled on them accidentally. The head of the Madrid library, embarrassed by the international attention that was drawn to the negligence of a long-dead shelver, lamely defended his institution by explaining that they would, in any case, have been discovered eventually.

Few errors of librarianship have such momentous consequences, and catalogers rarely have the responsibility of classifying and shelving materials of such value, but the incident in Madrid is a striking demonstration of the fact that an item misplaced is an item lost to the patrons of the library. The student unable to find a certain work of literary criticism, the teacher searching in vain for a filmstrip, and the who-done-it enthusiast asking for "another by the same author," find inadequate cataloging as frustrating as it was to the librarians in Madrid looking for the lost Leonardos.

There are information needs at each stage of life, from the pre-schooler developing listening skills during story hour to the elderly citizen seeking both recreational and informational materials. If, at any stage in the search, a seeker of information becomes frustrated, the library has failed in its purpose. Collections must be effectively organized so that patrons can find what has been selected for their use.

At first sight, modern cataloging practice may seem dauntingly complex. Information is now packaged in forms unknown a brief time ago; the rules of descriptive cataloging have been altered; and computer technology is changing cataloging processes even in small libraries. But these innovations have changed only the form, not the basic function of catalogs, which exist to guide users of library resources to the materials that answer their needs.

As librarians look forward to the information needs and technologies of the 21st century, the opportunities and challenges of their profession increase, as does the need for competent catalogers. Computers now make it possible to link all libraries, large and small, through their catalogs. Incorrect and illogical cataloging practice can impede the building of a vast information network. Today's catalogers may find themselves in almost any type of work environment, from being the only professional staff member, responsible for all library activities, to serving as part of a large cataloging team. Whatever the situation, a librarian with an understanding of basic terminology, cataloging principles, and practical application will find more professional challenges than ever before.

CHAPTER 1

THE CATALOG RECORD

CIVILIZATION began when the invention of writing made it possible for societies to record their knowledge. Once people learned that by drawing pictures or making stylus marks on clay they could keep track of such matters as taxes due or the correct form of religious rituals, the need for storing and organizing this information for future reference became obvious. Thus, as soon as libraries were established catalogers became a necessity, and early librarians, called by the Assyrians "men of the written tablets," had responsibilities very similar to those of catalogers today; that is, to create catalog records that answer questions about the authorship, subject, and location of library materials. Today's cataloger uses standard tools to prepare records so these questions are answered as accurately, consistently, and efficiently as possible.

LOCATING THE RECORD

Library users often come to the catalog with partial information about what they are seeking. They may know an author's first name (sometimes misspelled), or some significant words in the title, or they may have a vague notion of the subject area, but be unable to translate this into the terms used by catalogers. They may even find a relevant entry but become so confused at interpreting it they never find the item on the shelf. Catalogers try to anticipate users' problems, but this is not always easy to do.

The majority of those searching a library catalog are looking for an individual item. In order to give as much help as possible, the cataloger prepares records about each item under various HEADINGS that are filed, more or less alphabetically, in the catalog. These records are called ENTRIES, and the headings under which they are found are called ACCESS POINTS, because they provide the user with access to the record of the catalog (see Figure 1-1).

Headings do more, however, than locate individual items. They are standardized so that works having common characteristics are gathered together. These gatherings make it possible to identify all of an author's works in the collection, as well as a single title; or all materials on field hockey, not just a particular book. Headings provide access to a single title such as *The Rise of Theodore Roosevelt,* and also gather all the biographies of President Theodore Roosevelt together as a group.

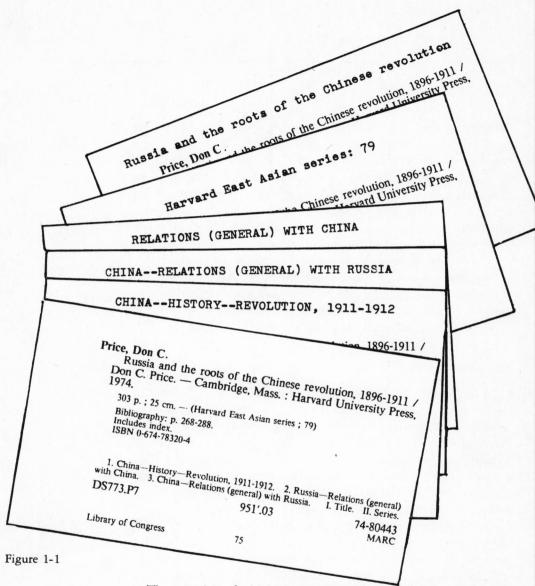

Russia and the roots of the Chinese revolution
Price, Don C. ...d the roots of the Chinese revolution, 1896-1911 /
...University Press,

Harvard East Asian series: 79

...the Chinese revolution, 1896-1911 /
...Harvard University Press,

RELATIONS (GENERAL) WITH CHINA

CHINA--RELATIONS (GENERAL) WITH RUSSIA

CHINA--HISTORY--REVOLUTION, 1911-1912

...ion 1896-1911 /

Price, Don C.
   Russia and the roots of the Chinese revolution, 1896-1911 /
Don C. Price. — Cambridge, Mass. : Harvard University Press,
1974.
   303 p. ; 25 cm. — (Harvard East Asian series ; 79)
   Bibliography: p. 268-288.
   Includes index.
   ISBN 0-674-78320-4

   1. China—History—Revolution, 1911-1912.   2. Russia—Relations (general)
with China.   3. China—Relations (general) with Russia.   I. Title.   II. Series.
DS773.P7
                                951'.03   74-80443
   Library of Congress   MARC
                                   75

Figure 1-1

The question of which are the most effective headings, or access
points, has long been the subject of debate among catalogers.
Headings for titles and for authors' names have been agreed upon,
but in certain cases the name of a corporate body takes the place of
a personal author. Other headings are selected primarily from those
BIBLIOGRAPHIC DETAILS found within the item itself, such as series
titles, joint authors, or performers. SUBJECT HEADINGS are customarily chosen by using a current edition of one of the standard tools
available for this purpose. The cataloger selects headings in the hope
that one will correspond with the user's prior knowledge of the
material. Entries are not made for physical characteristics, however,

and catalogs cannot help those who remember only the color of a book. It is interesting to note that when nonprint materials first began to appear in libraries, catalogers often assigned headings to types of format (*i.e.,* filmstrip), but as formats became more numerous this became impracticable. Many libraries today provide separate catalogs for their 16mm films, slides, or other media collections; others include their entire collection in a single file referred to as an OMNI CATALOG.

INTERPRETING THE RECORD

The catalog record provides a location symbol or CALL NUMBER, a description of the item, and selected access points. This basic data is often supplemented by other information. The record is laid out according to a uniform style that predetermines the arrangement of information and prevents, or at least limits, such questions as "Which is the call number?" or "Is this the title or the subject?"

The details of this record vary little from library to library. Bibliographic data is placed before physical description, and both are arranged in prescribed order. Notes may be added. ADDED ENTRIES and subject headings may be listed at the bottom as TRACINGS. Tracings indicate or "trace" additional headings or access points provided in the catalog for the particular item. When an item is withdrawn from the collection, it is important that all access points be removed from the catalog; tracings provide that information. In addition, the subject headings can serve to guide users to additional information. All librarians, whether or not they are catalogers, should be able to identify these elements whatever the format in which they are displayed; for however different entries may be arranged, the basic elements of a cataloging record do not differ.

Figure 1-2 shows a catalog record in card format. The tracing, indicated by Arabic number, tells the user there is a subject heading card filed under LANGUAGES, MODERN — STUDY AND TEACHING.

```
PB35   Chastain, Kenneth.
.G533      Toward a philosophy of second-language
       learning and teaching / by Kenneth Chastain ;
       foreword by Gilbert A. Jarvis. -- 1st ed.
       -- Boston, Mass. : Heinle & Heinle, c1980.
          ix, 115 p. ; 23 cm. -- (The Foreign and
       second language educator series)
          Includes bibliographies and index.

          1. Languages, Modern--Study and teaching.
       I. Jarvis, Gilbert A. II. Title.
```

Figure 1-2

ELEMENTS OF A CATALOGING RECORD

Call number	PB35 .G533
Main entry	Chastain, Kenneth (author's name)
Full title	Toward a philosophy of second-language learning and teaching
Statement of responsibility / author's name, added names associated with the work	by Kenneth Chastain ; foreword by Gilbert A. Jarvis
Edition statement	1st ed.
Publication, distribution information (place, publisher, date)	Boston, Mass. : Heinle & Heinle, c1980.
Physical description	ix, 115 p. ; 23 cm.
Series title	(The Foreign and second language educator series)
Notes (information added by cataloger)	Includes bibliographies and index.
Subject heading	Languages, Modern—Study and teaching
Added entries	I. Jarvis, Gilbert A. II. Title. (See full title given for entry.)

In the card catalog, subject headings are capitalized in order to distinguish them from added entries. In this illustration, there are also two added entries, indicated by Roman numerals, one under the name of Gilbert A. Jarvis, who wrote the foreword to this book. His name is on the title page and the cataloger felt that someone looking for the book might remember his name and use it as an access point. Someone remembering the title could find the book by looking for *Toward a Philosophy of Second-Language Learning and Teaching,* which is tracing II. The cataloger could have decided to provide an added entry under the series title (The Foreign and Second Language Educator Series), but in this case chose not to do so.

The entry in Figure 1-2 is called a MAIN ENTRY card. In the days when catalog cards were handwritten, catalogers usually prepared only one with complete bibliographic information. This full card, called the main entry, was filed under the author's name, or, when the work had no identifiable author, under the title. Brief or TRUNCATED RECORDS were copied for the subject heading cards and added entries.

When catalog cards began to be produced by automation, this distinction between the main entry card and other cards no longer strictly applied. It became a simple mechanical task to print complete information on all cards, and the user could find complete cataloging information no matter what access point—author, title, subject—was first consulted. The term has even less meaning today when a single cataloging record is entered in a computer database and a variety of access points are attached, any one of which will lead the user to the record. Now "main entry" generally refers to the form by which a work will be identified, not only in a library catalog, but also in single-entry bibliographies and other reference books.

Machine-readable cataloging records (records that can be stored and used by a computer) contain all of the bibliographic information libraries are accustomed to, and are prepared using the same standard tools. However, if the computer is to find the information in the database, it must be tagged so the computer can locate the appropriate record. For example, some sort of tag must be attached to each author's name. The computer can then be programmed to locate and display information attached to that TAG.

The Library of Congress realized in the 1950s that cataloging records distributed through computer tapes had great possibilities, but first standard tags had to be developed. The result was the first MARC (MAchine-Readable Cataloging) records. Today, there are several variations of the basic MARC and a variety of terms including MARC2, LCMARC, and USMARC. MARC is the generic term and USMARC is the term for MARC records created by the Library of Congress. Huge databases of cataloging records in the MARC format are now maintained. Because computers can communicate with each other, it is possible for many libraries to share these cataloging records through COMPUTER NETWORKS. These records, however, must be tagged by standard MARC format.

FULL MARC TAGGED DISPLAY

```
OCLC:  7163071       Rec stat:  c Entrd:   820605      Used:   880419
Type:  a Bib lvl: m Govt pub:     Lang:    eng Source:  Illus:
Repr:    Enc lvl:   Conf pub:  0 Ctry:    mau Dat top:s M/F/B:   10
Indx:  1 Mod rec:   Festschr:  0 Cont:    b
Desc:  a Int lvl:   Dates:   1980,
  1 010        82-111073//r86
  2 040        DLC $c DLC $d m/c
  3 050    0   P51 $b .C43
  4 082    0   401/.9 $2 19
  5 092        $b
  6 049        GAYM
  7 100   10   Chastain, Kenneth. $w cn
  8 245   10   Toward a philosophy of second-language learning and
teaching / $c by Kenneth Chastain ; foreword by Gilbert A. Jarvis
  9 250        1st ed.
 10 260    0   Boston, Mass. : $b Heinle & Heinle Publishers, $c c1980.
 11 300        ix, 115 p. ; $c 23 cm.
 12 440    0   Foreign & second language educator series.
 13 504        Includes bibliographies and index.
 14 650    0   Language and languages $x Study and teaching $x Addresses,
essays, lectures.
```

Figure 1-3

Figures 1-2 through 1-6 illustrate variations in the format of cataloging entries. Only the presentations differ; the information remains the same.

Figure 1-3 represents a full MARC record from the OCLC database. The first five lines represent FIXED FIELDS. A field in a computer database is a specified area where certain data is stored. A fixed field is one in which only a predetermined number of characters can be entered. The fixed fields in a MARC record offer the cataloger a chance to record such information as the language, date, or type of publication in hand.

The rest of the fields are VARIABLE FIELDS; that is, the number of characters in the field can vary from record to record. The MARC tags are the numbers to the left and indicate the elements of a catalog record.

Figure 1-4 represents an edited MARC record. Few catalog users need all the information stored in a full MARC record (see Figure 1-3), so most

EDITED MARC TAGGED DISPLAY

```
100  10 Chastain, Kenneth.
245  10 Toward a philosophy of second—language learning and teaching /
        *c by Kenneth Chastain ; foreword by Gilbert A. Jarvis.
250     1st ed.
260   0 Boston, Mass. : *b Heinle & Heinle, *c c1980.
300     ix, 115 p. ; *c 23 cm.
490   0 The Foreign and second language educator series.
504     Includes bibliographies and index.
650   0 Languages, Modern *x Study and teaching.
700  10 Jarvis, Gilbert A.
```

Figure 1-4

librarians will edit the record for their particular catalogs, retaining the information most useful to their patrons.

Figure 1-5 is the final record edited for display in an online catalog. MARC tags, which would make little sense to most users,

ONLINE CATALOG FORMATTED DISPLAY

```
LOCTN:  PUL GENERAL COLLECTION PB35 .C533
AUTHR:  Chastain, Kenneth.
TITLE:  Toward a philosophy of second—language learning and
        teaching / by Kenneth Chastain ; foreword by
        Gilbert A. Jarvis.
EDITN:  1st ed.
PUBLR:  Boston, Mass. : Heinle & Heinle, c1980.
DESCR:  ix, 115 p. ; 23 cm.
SUBJT:  Languages, Modern——Study and teaching.
```

Figure 1-5

have been replaced with words indicating the fields. The library's name and local call number have been added.

Figure 1-6 represents a record truncated by the computer. Such a record would be used when the entire bibliographic record is not required.

TRUNCATED RECORD

```
Screen 001 of 001
NMBR DATE
0001 1969  Toward a philosophy of education          Buford, Thomas D.,
0002 1980  Toward a philosophy of second-language learni Chastain, Kenneth,
0003 1982  Toward a philosophy of Zen Buddhism /        Izutsu, Toshihiko,
```

Figure 1-6

The main entry is normally under the author. However, when the item has no personal author, is the work of a group, or has been produced under editorial direction, the title serves as the main entry. The information is accessed by the first word of the title (disregarding the articles "a," "an," and "the"). To make the title stand out, a variation of form, called the HANGING INDENTION, is used. The first line consists of the title, and other descriptive details are indented below (see Figure 1-7).

```
The Second language curriculum / edited by Robert Keith
    Johnson. -- Cambridge [England] : New York :
    Cambridge University Press, 1989.
    xxii, 314 p.
    Bibliography: p. 286-309.

    1. Language and languages--Study and teaching.
2. Curriculum planning.
```

Figure 1-7

CREATING THE RECORD—A CATALOGER'S ART

From the earliest days, inventory records were kept of library materials housed in individual collections. For many centuries the primary role of librarians was to guard this stored material, and they were held officially responsible if any item was misplaced. Today many libraries still take annual inventories and report how many items have slipped away.

The file, or catalog, used to take this inventory is a list arranged in the order that materials are stored on the shelf, called the SHELF LIST. Since ancient times this type of record has been considered

FORMATTED DISPLAY ONLINE CATALOG

```
LOCTN:  PUL GENERAL COLLECTION P53.295 .S44 1989
TITLE:  The Second language curriculum / edited by Robert
        Keith Johnson.
PUBLR:  Cambridge [England] ; New York : Cambridge University
        Press, 1989.
DESCR:  xxii, 314 p. : ill.
NOTES:  Bibliography: p. 286-309.
SUBJT:  Language and languages—Study and teaching.
SUBJT:  Curriculum planning.
```

Figure 1-8

TAGGED DISPLAY: EDITED MARC

```
245  04  The Second language curriculum / #c edited by Robert Keith Johnson.
260  0   Cambridge [England] ; #a New York : #b Cambridge University Press,
         #c 1989.
263      8908
300      xxii, 314 p. : #b ill.
490  0   The Cambridge applied linguistics series.
500      Includes index.
504      Bibliography: p. 286-309.
650  0 Language and languages #x Study and teaching.
650  0 Curriculum planning.
```

Figure 1-9

essential. A small library might do without other records, but there should always be a shelf list record to answer the question "What materials are in this collection?"

Libraries of Babylonia and Assyria were far from small, however. They held thousands of clay tablets concerning subjects as diverse as taxation, law, literature, and religion. A simple shelf-list catalog was not adequate because it could not provide the answer to questions about the location of tablets on monument building or other specific topics. As a result, arrangement by subject was developed, and catalogs were kept for each subject. Call numbers were used to find these tablets; that is, each tablet was marked with a location symbol that was also recorded in the catalog listing. Works were further identified by title, and often annotations (brief descriptions of the contents) were added to the record. So, thousands of years ago, at Nineveh and Akkad, cataloging became an established art with records similar to those we now find in modern library catalogs.

During the 5th century AD, when the Roman Empire was destroyed by barbarian invaders, most libraries, including the great collection made by Constantine at Byzantium, were pillaged or left to decay. Fragments of classical libraries survived in churches and monasteries, and from these texts evolved the learning of the European renaissance. Some medieval and renaissance monastic and private libraries grew to considerable size, and manuscript catalogs in the form of books were produced to make their contents accessible to users. With few exceptions, these catalogs remained simple inventories with call numbers; not until the 17th century did cataloging under title and author's name become relatively common. The catalog of the Bodleian Library in Oxford, made in 1674, was probably the first to contain a shelf list, an alphabetical index of authors' names, and rudimentary classification by subject. Cataloging in the modern sense—providing access to materials by their authorship, title, subject, and form—was a creation of 19th-century librarians working in Britain, the United States, and Europe.

Since the third millennium BC, ways of preserving a permanent record of knowledge have evolved far beyond the papyrus roll and the clay tablet. One can now retrieve information from books, films, microforms, tapes, or computer discs, but librarians must still organize the materials in their collections so that similar information in a subject field is shelved together (CLASSIFICATION); give each item a prescribed shelf location (CALL NUMBERS); arrange items according to their subjects (SUBJECT HEADINGS); provide clear descriptions of materials so that they can be distinguished (DESCRIPTIVE CATALOGING); and keep an inventory of the collection (SHELF LIST).

According to the size and scope of the collection, some catalogs are more detailed and extensive than others. Before the invention of printing, books were copied by hand and the cost and laboriousness of this process limited the size of libraries. An inventory, or shelf list, was adequate for all but a few collections. This might still be true today in a small rental library, where patrons mainly browse for leisure reading. In special libraries, where users' requests are frequently answered with specific subject bibliographies, the emphasis is on subject analysis. In a rare book collection the careful description of valuable items is of prime importance. No matter what types of materials are collected, the cataloger must create cataloging records for them so that knowledge can be retrieved.

A CATALOGER'S TOOL KIT

If everyone were assigned to a particular library at birth, and could use only that library for their entire lifetime, there would be little need for cataloging tools. All libraries could be arranged differently without inconvenience to their users. In reality, however, people use many different libraries and media and information centers during their lives. Libraries share resources through interlibrary loan, and now have ways of linking collections together by computer networks. Consequently, there have been many efforts to standardize classification and cataloging procedures. Standard procedures allow librarians to catalog and organize collections, and readers to use them, in more than one library.

Classification

A standard classification schedule is essential for grouping materials within subject areas.

> Dewey, Melvil. *Abridged Dewey Decimal Classification and Relative Index*. Albany, NY: Forest Press, Division of OCLC Online Computer Library Center, Inc.
>
> Dewey, Melvil. *Dewey Decimal Classification and Relative Index*. Albany, NY: Forest Press, Division of OCLC Online Computer Library Center, Inc.
>
> *Library of Congress Classification Schedules: A Cumulation of Additions and Changes*. Detroit: Gale Research Company.
>
> Library of Congress. Subject Cataloging Division. *Classification*. 43 vols. Washington, DC: Library of Congress.

Most school and public libraries are arranged according to the Dewey Classification Schedules (DDC), and academic libraries according to the Library of Congress system (LCC). These numbers are part of the call number. Small general libraries commonly use the abridged version of Dewey.

Subject Headings

A standard subject heading list is used to select uniform headings so that the catalog can be used to locate particular topics.

> *Sears List of Subject Headings*. New York: The H. W. Wilson Company.
>
> Library of Congress, Subject Cataloging Division. *Library of Congress Subject Headings*. Washington, DC: Library of Congress.

Large collections and those using LC classification will use the LC Subject Headings list (LCSH). Small public and school libraries usually take their headings from *Sears*. Special collections devoted exclusively to acquisition of materials on a single topic, such as medicine or religion, often use uniform lists developed for that particular subject field.

Cataloging tools are updated according to various schedules, and sometimes partial updates appear before a new edition. Announcements and advertisements in professional journals alert catalogers to new editions.

Cataloging Codes

Items are described according to the precise specifications of a cataloging code so that they may be distinguished from one another. These rules provide guidance for recording bibliographic details such as names, titles, editions, and publishers; and for physical descriptions, such as number of pages, or size of film.

> *Anglo-American Cataloguing Rules.* (Second edition 1988 revision) Michael Gorman and Paul W. Winkler, eds. Chicago: American Library Association, 1988.

Using these basic tools, librarians can describe materials so that users can identify and select items from the catalog description (AACR2); can place items in shelf locations adjacent to other materials dealing with the same topic (DDC or LCC); and provide more precise subject access by using the standard subject heading list (*Sears* or LCSH).

In addition to these general tools, some libraries make use of other aids developed for special collections. For example, libraries that house only slides may follow more detailed rules for their descriptions; special collections in particular subject fields may use alternative subject heading lists; and a number of libraries have developed their own classification schemes or use other recognized systems like the Universal Dewey Classification. For the most part, however, the tools listed in this chapter are those commonly used in general collections.

A UNIT RECORD

When the Library of Congress began printing catalog cards for distribution to libraries it found that the simplest method was to print only one basic card, containing a complete bibliographic record, and to duplicate this card as needed to make all the entries in a unit. Thus each card, whether main or added entry, is a complete record. Libraries purchased cards in sets and typed headings of their choice in the space above the main entry.

Figure 1-10 shows a UNIT SET. The bibliographic record begins with the author's name as main entry. The cataloger has assigned two additional access points, title and one subject heading, so this unit comprises four cards: author, or main entry card; title, or added entry card; subject card; and shelf list card.

The cards in a unit set are filed alphabetically by whatever appears first at the top of the card, except for the shelf list card. In the example cited in Figure 1-10, *Media Selection Handbook* by Mary Robinson Sive will be filed in the S's under the author's last name. If the library owns other works by this author these too will be gathered in the catalog under Sive. Searches by title, *Media Selection Handbook,* will find it in the M's. The subject AUDIO-VISUAL MATERIALS is filed with other library materials with the same subject heading.

Shelf list records are arranged for the purpose of taking inventory and are normally available only to library staff. The shelf list consists

11

of duplicates of the main entry cards with individual designators added. In most cases the designator is the ACCESSION NUMBER, a number assigned to each item as it is acquired. In the example of a shelf list card in Figure 1-10, 31220 is the accession number; 31219 items were added to the library collection before this book was acquired. The ISBN (International Standard Book Number) 0-897287-350-1 is a unique number assigned by the publisher. Other unique numbers are added to the record: for example, 83-932 is the order number for this particular card set from the Library of Congress. These unique numbers are useful when identifying particular items in national bibliographic databases and should always be recorded on the shelf list card. The tracings indicate the headings the cataloger added to the record. Suggested call numbers from both DDC and LC schedules are also included.

The term MARC (machine-readable cataloging) indicates that this

Main Entry—Author

```
    Sive, Mary Robinson.
        Media selection handbook / Mary Robinson Sive.
    -- Littleton, Colo. : Libraries Unlimited, 1983.
        171 p. : ill. ; 24 cm.

        Includes bibliographical references and index.
        ISBN 0-897287-350-1 : $22.50


        1. Audio-visual materials--Catalogs.  I. Title.

    LB1043.Z9S58      1983              011          83-932
                                                      MARC
```

Added Entry—Title

```
    Media selection handbook

    Sive, Mary Robinson.
        Media selection handbook / Mary Robinson Sive.
    -- Littleton, Colo. : Libraries Unlimited, 1983.
        171 p. : ill. ; 24 cm.

        Includes bibliographical references and index.
        ISBN 0-897287-350-1 : $22.50


        1. Audio-visual materials--Catalogs.  I. Title.

    LB1043.Z9S58      1983              011          83-932
                                                      MARC
```

Figure 1-10

cataloging information is also available in machine-readable format.

With the exception of the accession number, which is a local number, this information has been supplied by the Library of Congress, and would not all be included in locally typed sets.

SUMMARY

Catalog entries consist of standardized records that include elements of information such as author, title, publisher, date, and physical characteristics. These records, or entries about individual items, are gathered together under headings, or access points, so that materials may be seen singly or as part of a group of works having certain features in common.

Elements are placed on catalog cards in a prescribed and consistent arrangement. This arrangement may alter according to

Subject Entry

```
     AUDIO-VISUAL MATERIALS--CATALOGS

Sive, Mary Robinson.
   Media selection handbook / Mary Robinson Sive.
-- Littleton, Colo. : Libraries Unlimited, 1983.
   171 p. : ill. ; 24 cm.

   Includes bibliographical references and index.
   ISBN 0-897287-350-1 : $22.50


   1. Audio-visual materials--Catalogs.  I. Title.

LB1043.Z9S58    1983          011        83-932
                                           MARC
```

Shelf List Card

```
   Sive, Mary Robinson.
      Media selection handbook / Mary Robinson Sive.
   -- Littleton, Colo. : Libraries Unlimited, 1983.
      171 p. : ill. ; 24 cm.

      Includes bibliographical references and index.
      ISBN 0-897287-350-1 : $22.50
      31220

      1. Audio-visual materials--Catalogs.  I. Title.


   LB1043.Z9S58    1983          011        83-932
                                              MARC
```

Figure 1-10 (continued)

the format of the catalog, but the elements themselves vary only in minor respects. When users become familiar with these bibliographic elements, they are more successful in finding information in the catalog.

The cataloger's art is to create records for a collection so that specific information can be retrieved on demand. Standard tools are used in their preparation so that libraries may share records, and users find information in many libraries.

CHAPTER REVIEW

Terms to understand:

access points	ISBN
accession numbers	LCSH
added entries	main entry
bibliographic details	MARC
call numbers	omni catalog
classification	shelf list
computer network	subject headings
descriptive cataloging	tag
entries	tracings
fixed field	truncated record
hanging indention	unit set
headings	variable field

Functions of the catalog record:

1. Shelf list provides for inventory
2. Call numbers locate items on the shelf
3. Classification through notation
4. Subject heading locates subjects by specific topics
5. Descriptive cataloging identifies and describes individual items

Cataloger's tools:

Anglo-American Cataloguing Rules (AACR2)
Dewey Decimal Classification and Relative Index and *Abridged Dewey Decimal Classification and Relative Index*
Library of Congress Classification Schedules
Sears List of Subject Headings
Library of Congress Subject Headings

CHAPTER 2

STORING THE RECORD—LIBRARY CATALOGS

THE CATALOG'S FORM

ALTHOUGH the basic information found in a catalog record has varied little over time, the form of the library's catalog has varied widely since ancient days. Library catalogs tend to change physical form whenever technology allows another format to be made that is more efficient or less expensive.

Assyrian inventories were made on clay tablets, Egyptian records were carved on the library walls, medieval collections were listed in BOOK CATALOGS, and during the 19th century CARD CATALOGS became popular. Today, the computer has made it possible to store records in MICROFORM CATALOGS, ONLINE COMPUTER CATALOGS, and CD-ROM CATALOGS. The idea of a UNION CATALOG, a listing of the holdings of more than one library collection, first proposed during the 13th century, has now been replaced by NETWORKING, that is, electronic access to online catalogs scattered throughout the nation.

Although the card is not the oldest form, it has certainly been the most popular. Its advantages were first recognized at the end of the 18th century in France, when the revolutionary government confiscated large numbers of books from private collections and church libraries. Descriptions of these books made according to the French National Code of 1791 were entered on slips of paper and playing cards in regional centers and mailed to the National Library in Paris, where they were arranged alphabetically by author and fastened together by a cord passed through the lower left-hand corner. This system, which allowed catalogers to interpolate or remove accessions without disturbing the catalog as a whole, did not become widely accepted until the late 19th century. When, in 1902, the Library of Congress began selling sets of printed catalog cards for a nominal fee, book catalogs rapidly disappeared in the United States, and, although other forms were still used for special purposes, the card catalog prevailed.

The decision of the Library of Congress to sell cards had more important consequences than the disappearance of book catalogs. Until then, cataloging had been done by librarians who worked more or less independently and made little effort to standardize procedures. Now there was a central agency providing not only printed cards, but also standards for the cataloging of every library.

The Card Catalog

15

The cataloging practices of the Library of Congress therefore became the cataloging standards for most libraries. The Library of Congress continues to exert a strong influence to this day.

In those early years the disadvantages of card catalogs had not yet been realized. Although card catalogs grow slowly, they may reach enormous proportions in large collections, and even small libraries found space at a premium as they tried to position the card catalog for the convenience of both the public and the library staff. Catalogs often double in size every 20 years or less. They have to be housed in specially designed furniture and require expensive maintenance as cards are added, removed, shifted, and altered. A visit to any large collection that had a card catalog revealed a number of staff members doing little else but keeping it up to date. Furthermore, during the social unrest of the late 1960s and '70s, card catalogs proved especially vulnerable to attack by those who expressed their radical opinions by removing and destroying drawers of catalog cards.

The Book Catalog

Listing the contents of a library in a ledger or notebook was one of the earliest methods of keeping an inventory. When technology allowed this information to be printed, rather than handwritten, book catalogs became standard. Produced in multiple copies, they were used for inventory, and for interlibrary loan. As long as library collections grew slowly, book catalogs remained serviceable, but, as the French National Library discovered, they became inadequate once a collection had begun to grow rapidly. It is costly and difficult to produce new editions or update with supplements.

Book catalogs came into general use once again when, during the late 1960s, it became possible to print them easily and inexpensively by computer. By then card catalogs were causing space problems in many libraries and computer-produced book catalogs gained in popularity. It is possible to print a complete computer catalog for every branch library, even for each bookmobile, and copies can be shelved in classrooms, offices, and homes. Mutilation or loss of a volume is less problematic, because new ones can be printed and maintenance costs are relatively low. Cataloging records can be truncated and made simpler for the general public to use—an impractical idea when the card catalog served as the main bibliographic tool for user and librarian alike. Book catalogs can be photocopied to provide students with a complete list of titles in a subject area; and circulation has been found to increase when whole pages of material, rather than one item at a time, can be scanned at once. Many predicted that the book catalog would enjoy a revival during the 1980s, but technology moves quickly, and although many libraries, particularly public libraries, still rely on their book catalogs, other computer-produced forms have entered the field.

A microform is a miniature photographic reproduction of printed works, blueprints, diagrams, or cataloging information that must be enlarged for reading with magnifying equipment. Two common forms are MICROFICHE, a sheet of transparent film, usually 4×6 inches, containing a number of images arranged in rows, and MICROFILM, a roll of transparent film, containing images arranged in a sequence. Either of these forms may be directly produced from a computer database, creating a computer output microform catalog, or COM CAT.

Computer Output Microform Catalog

COM catalogs offer many advantages: compactness, multiple copies, multiple entry display, low maintenance, and low cost. The cost of reissuing the entire catalog is low because there is no need to produce printed copy. Even those librarians who have moved on to interactive catalogs often maintain COM catalogs for their users and staff, or as backup to computer down-time.

An INTERACTIVE CATALOG connects the user directly to the information source (machine-readable catalog records stored in a computer DATABASE). Normally, the computer provides very rapid access to the records, which can be called up from a number of access points. Interactive catalogs have many of the advantages of the COM and book catalogs. Terminals can be placed in the library or in remote locations. The user can view a number of records at one time and make copies easily. Computer catalogs are compact, can be instantly updated, and eliminate the need for the constant manual filing, removal, or sorting of cards required by the card catalog. But the principal advantage of an electronic catalog is its ability to interact with the user.

Interactive Catalogs

Online computer catalogs were the first interactive catalogs found in libraries. In an online catalog, the user is connected directly to library files, which are stored in a computer. Obviously, to provide an online catalog a library must have its records in machine-readable format, access to a computer, enough terminals and ways to connect them to the computer, and a backup for computer down-time.

Online Computer Catalogs

CD-ROM (compact disc, read-only-memory) is an optically based medium with massive storage capacity. Played by a drive attached to a computer, the disc is encoded permanently and is remastered when more records are added. A formatted CD-ROM can be searched in the interactive mode without the communication cost of an online system. CD-ROM cannot, however, be up-dated instantly like an online catalog, but must be reformatted periodically like a COM or book catalog.

CD-ROM Catalog

17

Electronic catalogs can be searched so rapidly that users can modify a search if they are not finding the records they require. The user can create searches by combining terms; for example, author, title, and subject can be linked together into one search statement, several subjects can be linked together, or keywords from any field in the catalog entry can serve as access points. "Help" screens offer instant assistance to users having difficulty with the system. No wonder users indicate a high level of satisfaction with interactive catalogs.

ORGANIZING THE RECORDS

No matter what the physical form of the catalog, all entries must be arranged in a logical manner. Computer professionals speak of "logical files" and certainly retrieval is difficult unless one understands the system in which records are stored.

Early catalogs were often inventory lists, usually filed in order of acquisition; but catalogers soon experimented with other arrangements. One popular early arrangement by subject, or topic, now known as a CLASSED CATALOG, is unsuitable for author or title searches. When arranged by call numbers, the shelf list resembles a classed catalog because it groups materials by subject.

During the late 19th century, a more sophisticated kind of catalog, the DICTIONARY CATALOG, was introduced. In this catalog all entries, whether author, title, or subject, are filed together within a single alphabet. The dictionary catalog offers users complete access to the collection from a single file. It also presents problems, particularly in large collections, because the sheer size and number of entries under one term or name can be overwhelming. To alleviate these problems, and to simplify filing, many libraries use a DIVIDED CATALOG. This consists of two files, one for main and added entries, the other for subjects. Both dictionary and divided catalogs exist in the form of cards, books, and microforms.

Computer files are organized according to a certain logic. When catalog records are organized in a bibliographic database, each record is stored once, rather than many times as in a card catalog. The standard format for representing the library cataloging is MARC. Then a series of files or indices are created to provide access to each record. Minimal access points should be those available in a card catalog. AACR2 remains the standard for preparing the record.

SUMMARY

Catalog records may be stored in a number of ways, but no matter what its form, the library catalog will continue to answer basic questions about the collection, providing users with information about what is available and where it can be found. The cataloger must organize a collection of knowledge into a logical system, so that specific information can be retrieved on demand. No matter what the form of the catalog itself, the records are still prepared using the basic standards. In fact, if librarians are to network, it becomes even more important to provide standard access points.

CHAPTER REVIEW

Terms to understand:

book catalog	interactive catalog
card catalog	microfiche catalog
CD-ROM catalog	microfilm catalog
classed catalog	microform catalog
COM catalog	networking
database	online computer catalog
dictionary catalog	union catalog
divided catalog	

CHAPTER 3

CATALOGING CODES: FROM CUTTER TO AACR2

EVERY ITEM in a collection should be identified and described. The basic cataloger's tool for this task is a standard code. Several codes have been written over the years, and, just as the forms of the catalog have changed with technology, so codes have come and gone, each reflecting the information needs of the time in which it was created.

PANIZZI AND CUTTER

The foundations of modern cataloging were laid during the mid-19th century, when the rapid growth of public collections created a need for the organization and classification of books and documents. Early cataloging codes were written with the needs of a particular library in mind, although each built, where it could, upon ideas borrowed from others. One influential code was developed at the British Museum by an Italian refugee, Antonio (later Sir Anthony) Panizzi, who was appointed Keeper of Printed Books in 1837, and Principal Librarian in 1856. Panizzi perceived the importance of a catalog to study and research, and devised a code of 91 rules by which the British Museum catalog, first issued between 1881 and 1900, was created. This pioneering work was continued by an American, Charles Cutter, who served as librarian of the Boston Athenaeum from 1868. Having produced a five-volume catalog of his library, Cutter wrote *Rules for a Printed Dictionary Catalogue* (1876), a code so well formulated that it has influenced modern codes.

In his preface Cutter identified three main objectives for a library catalog:

1. To enable a person to find a book of which either author, title, or subject is known.

2. To show what the library has by a given author, on a given subject, or in a given kind of literature.

3. To assist in the choice of a book: as to its edition (bibliographically), or as to its character (literary or topical).

The catalog, in Cutter's view, should not only help the user identify individual works, but also distinguish between editions, and gather items by the same author, on the same subject, or in the same literary genre. These aims could only be achieved by ensuring that new entries were made on the same principles as those already in place. As materials were cataloged, each entry was checked to make sure the information was correctly and consistently given. Authors may marry, divorce, add and drop initials, adopt pen names, or otherwise create confusion. Titles may vary from one edition of a work to another and corporate bodies may change their names. Catalogers therefore do not simply record what appears on the title page, but research and assign UNIFORM HEADINGS for authors, corporations, series, and sometimes titles. Libraries maintain AUTHORITY FILES, a list of headings already in use, so that catalogers can check every entry before completing the record. By observing these procedures, Cutter's second objective can be attained and the catalog can answer such questions as "How many books do you have by Victoria Holt?" or "How many editions of *Alice in Wonderland* are in the library?"

During the development of a library catalog, however, a number of codes may have been followed and even a small catalog can be confusing for this reason. Cutter hoped that codes would provide for "the convenience of the public" by indicating entry choices most likely to be used by the "class of people who use the library." If, following different codes, entries are made under "Clemens, Samuel Langhorn" at one time and under "Twain, Mark" the next; or suddenly switched from place of location to entry under the name of the institution (e.g., "New York. State University," to "State University of New York"), Cutter's hopes for a convenient catalog are dashed.

The lesson to be drawn from this is that the reply, "Look in the catalog," in response to a user's request for assistance is often not a useful answer. Because codes and cataloging rules have changed, even the smallest catalog can be difficult to use, and although interactive catalogs can offer users who are unfamiliar with standard access points entry through keywords or terms, it is still possible, if consistent standards are ignored, for items to elude the user.

AFTER CUTTER

By the 1960s cataloging codes, often the complex products of committees, were in urgent need of reexamination. Seymour Lubetzky of the Library of Congress, who was selected for this task, suggested a return to Cutter's principles, and examined existing rules in their light. Lubetzky became the first editor of *Anglo-American Cataloguing Rules* (AACR), which was issued in 1967 and generally accepted by British, Canadian, and American libraries. Although AACR1 recognized the growing importance of non-book materials such as filmstrips, the rapid proliferation of new formats and the effect of technology on the form of the catalog soon called for a revised code. *Anglo-American Cataloguing Rules, Second Edition* (AACR2), edited by Paul Winkler and Michael Gorman, was published in 1978 and formally adopted for international use in 1981. During the ten years following the publication of AACR2 the rules were generally adopted in most English-speaking countries and translated into many languages, including Japanese and Urdu. Cataloging rules cannot remain static, however, because technology changes, some rules prove inadequate, and questions of ambiguous wording arise. Three sets of rule revisions were published between 1982 and 1985, and in 1987 a draft revision of Chapter 9, "Computer Files," appeared. These revisions were incorporated into AACR2, 1988 revision. However, the basic principles, structure, and philosophy remain the same.

When AACR1 was published, it was predicted to be the last code written for the card form of a catalog, and this has indeed been the case. Use of the card catalog has declined as more and more information has been stored in computer databases and transmitted to users by terminals or on microform. Even the terminology of cataloging has changed. Access is gained to a database via an access point, not through main or added entries, and whereas earlier codes discussed "Choice of Entry," AACR2 contains a chapter called "Choice of Access Points."

Cataloging practice has not only been changed by the computer, but also by an increase in the number of nonbook formats acquired by libraries, such as video tapes, games, kits, and computer disks, as well as films and recordings. This innovation has had an especially pronounced effect on school libraries, many of which have been renamed "media centers." Among the cataloging difficulties presented by these new materials is the problem of assigning an author entry to items such as films that are created by several people. Main entry under title has therefore become more common in the present code, and the term author has been more strictly defined.

During the 1960s rapid progress was made in establishing international cataloging standards. A group representing major nations and languages that met in Paris in 1961 formulated guidelines called the Paris Principles, which were prefaced, like Cutter's rules, by a statement of the functions of the catalog. Descriptive cataloging was reformed by the publication of *International Standard Bibliographic Description* (ISBD) in 1974. This was an international format for description of books that could be understood and filed into the catalogs of other countries and converted into machine-readable form. Rules for other forms of material were promised. If cataloging was to reflect international practice it needed to be incorporated in the code.

During this same period North American publishers began to assign an individual number to each edition of a work. The

International Standard Book Number (ISBN) and the *International Standard Serial Number* (ISSN) are now printed routinely in a prominent place in most books, magazines, and a growing number of other types of materials. These numbers provide another means of identifying and accessing individual titles.

The code is divided into two parts, corresponding to the two basic purposes of the catalog. Part 1, DESCRIPTION, states the rules for bibliographic and physical description of individual items and is based on the ISBD formats. Part 2, HEADINGS, UNIFORM TITLES AND REFERENCES, provides guidance in the choice of standard headings and access points in order to gather materials together by common bibliographic elements. This organization follows the order in which catalogers work. In Part 1, the cataloger will find guidance for describing the item in hand and prepares that part of the card shaded in Figure 3-1. (Note addition of the ISBN in the note area.)

AACR2

```
Comanor, William S.
    Advertising and market power / William S. Comanor
and Thomas A. Wilson. -- Cambridge, Mass. : Harvard
University Press, 1974.
    xvi., 257 p. : ill. ; 25 cm. -- (Harvard economic
studies ; v. 144)
    Includes bibliographical references and index.
    ISBN 0-674-00580-5


    1. Advertising. I. Wilson, Thomas Arthur, 1935-
joint author  II. Title  III. Series

HF5827.C587              659.1           73-90849
Library of Congress      74 [4]          MARC
```

Figure 3-1

Part 2 provides rules for the selection of standard headings and access points, given in those portions of the card that are shaded in figure 3-2.

The editors of AACR2 anticipated that the appearance of new formats after the publication of their book would create a need for more rules and they left chapters 14 through 20 blank to accommodate them. AACR2 contains rules for the description of books, cartographic materials, manuscripts, music, sound recordings, motion pictures and video recordings, graphic materials (including filmstrips), computer files, three-dimensional artifacts and realia, microforms, and serials. Although their aim is to standardize cataloging procedures, the editors recognize that "uniform legislation for all types and sizes of catalogs is neither possible nor

```
Comanor, William S.
   Advertising and market power / William S. Comanor
and Thomas A. Wilson. —— Cambridge, Mass. : Harvard
University Press, 1974.
   xvi., 257 p. : ill. ; 25 cm. —— (Harvard economic
studies ; v. 144)
   Includes bibliographical references and index.
   ISBN 0-674-00580-5


   1. Advertising  I. Wilson, Thomas Arthur, 1935—
joint author II. Title III. Series
```

Figure 3-2

desirable," and encourage "the application of individual judgment based on specific local knowledge." It is necessary for the cataloger to develop a sense of local priorities in order to make appropriate cataloging decisions.

SUMMARY

Cataloging codes are important because they determine the structure of the catalog and, ultimately, the users' success in retrieving information. Following a standard code also makes it possible for libraries to share materials and allows patrons to use the catalog of any library. In 1876 Charles Cutter identified two major purposes of the catalog: to locate an individual work, and to gather or relate works that share bibliographic characteristics. Librarians still try to achieve Cutter's objectives. Today, librarians are called upon to catalog all manner of items from collections of geological specimens to rare books, and to provide bibliographic information that can be internationally understood. AACR2 was developed in the effort to meet such challenges. Part 1 helps the cataloger describe an individual item to meet one main objective of the catalog; Part 2 makes it possible to assign standard access points that will gather certain works together.

CHAPTER REVIEW

Terms to understand:

Anglo-American Cataloguing Rules, rev. ed. (AACR2)
authority file
International Standard Bibliographic Description (ISBD)
International Standard Book Number (ISBN)
International Standard Serial Number (ISSN)
uniform heading

Purpose of the catalog:

To enable a person to find a book of which author, title, or subject
is known.

To show what the library has by a given author, on a given subject,
or in a given kind of literature.

To assist in the choice of a book.

AACR2 *provides:*

Cataloging rules for various formats, including rules for describing
materials and assigning access points.

ISBD punctuation.

CHAPTER 4

DESCRIBING THE ITEM: AACR2, PART I

DESCRIPTIVE CATALOGING has become more multifarious as formats have proliferated. Part 1 of AACR2, entitled DESCRIPTION, provides rules for this part of the cataloging process.

CONCEPTS OF DESCRIPTION

Rules for description are based on five principles:
a) The elements of description
b) Punctuation
c) Sources of information
d) Levels of description
e) Standard terminology

The Elements of Description

The description of an item is divided into eight areas, known as the elements of description:

Title and statement of responsibility
Edition
*Material (or type of publication) specific details
Publication, distribution, etc.
Physical description
Series
Notes
Standard number and terms of availability
*(Applicable only to cartographic materials, serials, computer files and printed music)

Except for the addition of the standard numbers (ISBN and ISSN), these are the elements catalogers have normally recorded in the past. When library materials consisted primarily of books, however, the publication and distribution area was known as the imprint and the physical description area as the collation. To prepare an entry these elements are first located and identified in the item being cataloged.

Punctuation

The current system of punctuation (ISBD) is an international creation, developed to assist the conversion of cataloging information into machine-readable form. Use of this punctuation and sequence makes it possible to identify each element as it appears in the descriptive record even when the language in which the entry is written is not known to the cataloger.

Although ISBD punctuation may look strange to the uninitiated, it is relatively easy to master. The eight elements are separated by a full stop, indicated by a period, a space, an em dash (—), and a space. Because most typewriters do not have an em dash, use two hyphens instead (– –). Unless starting a new paragraph, separate all elements of the description by full stops.

Other punctuation may be required within elements, and this is demonstrated as each is discussed.

Catalogers should not only follow common principles in recording elements, they should also derive their information from the same parts of the materials. If one cataloger consults the book jacket or the filmstrip box, whereas another uses the book's title page or the label on the film can, they are unlikely to produce identical descriptions. When cataloging books, turn first to the title and copyright pages, where bibliographic information will be found. The title page is now a standard convention, with certain information routinely printed on the back (VERSO) as well as the front of that page. This is not the case in many other formats, such as games or realia, which have no comparable convention. The code gives catalogers a standard to use by identifying a CHIEF SOURCE OF INFORMATION for each format, along with acceptable secondary sources. The Chief Source of Information is the first place to look when preparing to record the elements of description.

Sources of Information

Early catalog codes were created primarily for use in large collections where it was assumed that readers were interested in full bibliographic description. Printed Library of Congress cards follow this practice. Because many libraries do not need complete descriptive details, there is a demand for "short," "medium," and "full" cataloging that is supplied to some extent by commercial vendors of simplified cataloging copy. AACR2 was the first widely accepted code to recognize this need.

AACR2 allows a choice among three levels of description: from First Level, the minimum amount of information, to Third Level, the most detailed. In some libraries, it is sufficient to record the number of pages or type of film. Others include not only the number of pages, but the height of the book; not only the type of film, but also the running time. AACR2 encourages catalogers to make decisions about the level of description according to the information needs of users.

Levels of Description

Standard
Terminology

As formats have multiplied it has become necessary to tell users whether a work such as *Hamlet* takes the form of a film, a video tape, a sound recording, or a printed text. To ensure that the terms used to describe these formats do not vary, AACR2 provides standard terminology.

Some libraries maintain a separate catalog for each format; others list all materials in an omni catalog. For users of omni catalogs AACR2 provides the option of a GENERAL MATERIAL DESIGNATION [GMD], which is given in brackets immediately after the title proper. The GMD alerts users to the general physical class to which an item belongs; e.g., Christmas oratorios [sound recording]; The Search for solutions [motion picture]. When a library decides to use this option, the cataloger selects the correct term from either the British or the North American list (see Figure 4-1). These general terms are further clarified in the physical description area of the record.

These five principles of description are important in the construction of a bibliographic record. The *elements of description* are areas included in an entry, appearing in a prescribed order. ISBD *punctuation* highlights each of these elements. *Sources of information* determine where one looks for them on the item being cataloged. *Levels of description* depend on the needs of a library. *Standard terminology* ensures that the various formats will be referred to in consistent terms.

GENERAL MATERIAL DESIGNATIONS

British Terms	North American and Australian Terms	
LIST 1	LIST 2	microform
braille	art original	microscope slide
cartographic material	art reproduction	model
computer file	braille	motion picture
graphic	chart	music
manuscript	computer file	picture
microform	diorama	realia
motion picture	filmstrip	slide
multimedia	flash card	sound recording
music	game	technical drawing
object	globe	text
sound recording	kit	toy
text	manuscript	transparency
videorecording	map	videorecording

Figure 4-1

CONSTRUCTING THE ENTRY

The cataloger cannot construct an entry until format, Chief Source of Information, and level of description have been determined. These steps follow in logical order:

Step One   Determine the format and the Chief Source of Information.

Step Two   Determine the level of description.

Step Three   Identify and record the descriptive elements.

Step One. *Determine the format of the item, and the Chief Source of Information.*

The cataloger first decides what type of material is being cataloged and which rules apply. There are rules for description of the following formats:

books, pamphlets, and printed sheets
cartographic materials
manuscripts
music
sound recordings
motion picture and videorecordings
graphic materials (including filmstrips and photos)
computer files
three-dimensional artifacts and realia
microforms
serials

In most cases, decisions about format are easily made, and only multimedia sets present difficulties. The kind of format determines the Chief Source of Information.

Once the format of the material is decided, the cataloger examines the correct sources of information on that item. This is an important step, because it is possible for items to have one title on the spine or jacket, and another on a label, or for dates and names to vary. Figure 4-2 lays out the sources of information for each format.

The initial examination is often called TECHNICAL READING. This is not a full reading or viewing, but a process of identifying the pieces of information that make up the elements of description for the item in hand. The Chief Source of Information is the first place to look, and if the technical reading reveals that titles or dates differ within an item then the information in the Chief Source should be followed.

Information on the item itself frequently differs from that on the package or accompanying material. For example, a sound recording may have one title on the jacket and another on the label. In this case, the title on the label (the Chief Source of Information for sound recordings) is the title used by the cataloger for the catalog record. If there are several Chief Sources, choose the one with the latest date of publication. If none applies to the entire item, such as a textbook series with a title page for each level, or a sound recording with different labels on each side, treat them all as if they were a single source.

When the Chief Source is missing, or is inadequate, the other sources are consulted in descending order. For example, according to the chart the Chief Source of Information for a microfilm is the title frame. If no title frame exists, accept information from the following places: 1) the rest of the item 2) the container 3) accompanying printed materials or 4) another source. Often details such as dates are not given on the sound recording label, but can be identified somewhere on the jacket. Thus, when no date exists on the Chief Source, take any date found on other acceptable sources. In general, information found on the item itself should be preferred to information given elsewhere, either in accompanying material or on the packaging. Only rarely do catalogers supply details, and these are always clearly distinguished by enclosing them in brackets.

Step Two. *Determine the level of description.*

The level of description determines which descriptive details will appear in the final record. Not all items in a collection may need records of equal detail, so libraries need not adopt one level or another consistently. A library can choose a level and describe all materials by this standard. Others may decide on the level of detail according to the nature of the item being cataloged and the information needs of those most likely to use it.

First Level of Description

For First Level of Description include at least the basic elements with a few additional details (see Figure 4-3). Observe the full stop between each element, and other punctuation used within each area. Note that First Level is a standard record and, unlike a truncated record, it contains the basic elements with additional details. It can be expanded into a fuller record if necessary.

1st paragraph

Title proper / first statement of responsibility, if different from main entry heading in form or number or if there is no main entry heading. -- Edition statement. -- Material (or type of publication) specific details. -- First publisher, etc., date of publication.

SOURCES OF INFORMATION

Where to look for Descriptive Elements	BOOKS, PAMPHLETS, AND PRINTED SHEETS	CARTOGRAPHIC MATERIALS
CHIEF SOURCE OF INFORMATION	Title page	A) Cartographic item itself B) Container or case, cradle and stand
Alternative Sources	If there is no chief source, take that part of the item that supplies the most information. (Cover, half-title page, colophon, etc.)	If information is not available from the chief source, take it from any accompanying material.

Where to look for Descriptive Elements	MUSIC	SOUND RECORDINGS
CHIEF SOURCE OF INFORMATION	Use as the chief source of information whichever—title page, the cover, or the caption—furnishes the fullest information.	TYPE CHIEF SOURCE Disc Label (attached to disc) Tape (open reel-to-reel) Reel and label

Alternative Sources	If there is no chief source, take from the following (in order of preference):
	  caption
	  cover
	  colophon
	  other preliminaries or other sources
		Tape cassette Cassette and label
		Tape cartridge Cartridge and label
		Roll Label
		Sound recording on film Container and label
		
		Treat accompanying textual material on a container as the chief source if it supplies a collective title, and the parts do not.

Where to look for Descriptive Elements	MOTION PICTURES AND VIDEO RECORDINGS	GRAPHIC MATERIALS
CHIEF SOURCE OF INFORMATION	The film itself (e.g., the title frames) and its container (and its label) if the container is an integral part of the item (e.g., a cassette).	The item itself including any labels permanently affixed and a container that is an integral part. If of two or more physical parts, treat the container that is the unifying element as the chief source if it supplies a collective title.
Alternative Sources	If no chief source, take from the following: accompanying textual material (e.g., scripts, short lists, publicity items)	If no chief source, take from the following (in order of preference): container (box, frame, etc.) accompanying textual material (manuals, leaflets) other sources

Figure 4-2

31

SOURCES OF INFORMATION

Where to look for Descriptive Elements	COMPUTER FILES	THREE-DIMENSIONAL ARTIFACTS AND REALIA
CHIEF SOURCE OF INFORMATION	The title screen or a container furnishing a collective title.	The object itself, together with any accompanying textual material and container issued by publisher or manufacturer of item.
Alternative Sources	If no user label, take from the following (in order of preference): documentation issued by creator or producer information printed on the container	
	Prefer information available from internal sources	Prefer information found on the object itself (including affixed labels) to information found in accompanying textual materials or on the container.

Where to look for Descriptive Elements	MICROFORMS		SERIALS
CHIEF SOURCE OF INFORMATION	TYPE	CHIEF SOURCE	The title page of the first issue or the first issue that is available.
	Microfilm	Title frame	
	Aperture cards	Case for the set, the title card, or if a single card, the card itself	If no chief source, take from the following (in order of preference): cover caption masthead editorial pages colophon other pages
	Microfiche and Micro-opaques	Title frame	
	If information is presented on successive frames or cards, treat these all as the chief source.		
Alternative Sources	If no chief source, take from the following (in order of preference): rest of the item, including container container accompanying eye-readable material any other source		If information traditionally given on the title pages is given on facing pages, treat the two pages as the title page.

Figure 4-2 (continued)

2nd paragraph	Extent of item (physical description)
3rd paragraph	Note(s)
Above Tracing	Standard number

The first statement of responsibility should be omitted when it is identical to the main entry at the head of the record. Place of publication and series information are also omitted. When these details are considered important they can be included in the First Level. For instance, place of publication might be omitted as a general rule, but included when the publisher is a local company.

The Second Level of Description includes more details (see Figure 4-3). Statements of responsibility are expanded to include all those with creative responsibility mentioned in the Chief Source of Information, for example: translators, editors, and illustrators. Place of publication is included and the physical details are augmented with dimensions and other data concerning the appearance of the item. Series information is fully given. The record becomes longer and more definite. | **Second Level of Description**

1st paragraph	Title proper [general material designation] = Parallel title : other title information / first statement of responsibility ; each subsequent statement of responsibility
	— edition statement / first statement of responsibility relating to the edition
	— material (or type of publication) specific details
	— first place of publication, etc. : first publishers, etc., date of publication, etc.
2nd paragraph	Extent of item : other physical details ; dimensions — (Title proper of series / statement of responsibility relating to series, ISSN of series ; numbering within the series. Title of subseries, ISSN of subseries ; numbering within subseries)

3rd paragraph	Note(s)
Above Tracing	Standard number

Note the punctuation used within each element. A slash separates title information from statements of responsibility. Colons separate places from publishers, and series information is put in parentheses. As noted, use of the GMD is optional, and usually is determined by the library's cataloging policy.

Third Level of Description

The Third Level of Description is usually lengthy because it includes all elements that are applicable. Nothing is omitted: names associated with the work, publishers, distributors, series information, and physical details are included, whether considered essential information or not. Cataloging at this level is not common and is usually applied to material locally produced.

LEVELS OF CATALOGING

Level One

```
Davidson, Audrey.
     Substance and manner. -- Hiawatha Press,
1977.
     103 p.

     Includes bibliographical references.

     ISBN 0-930276-01-9
```

Level Two

```
Davidson, Audrey.
     Substance and manner : studies in music
and the other arts / by Audrey Davidson ;
preface by Herbert M. Scheuller. -- St. Paul,
Minn. : Hiawatha Press, 1977.
     xii, 103 p. : music ; 23 cm.
     Includes bibliographical references.

     ISBN 0-930276-01-9
```

Figure 4-3

How does the cataloger select an appropriate level? If a library draws up guidelines for the use of all three levels, these points should be taken into consideration.

1. The information needs of library users. For example, place of publication is often required for students preparing bibliographies and can be added to First Level although it would ordinarily be omitted.

2. The availability of staff and other resources for cataloging activities. When the staff has little time for cataloging, First Level provides a basic standard description and meets the needs of those searching for popular reading materials. On those rare occasions when a missing bibliographic detail is needed, a common reference tool can supply it. Those libraries that catalog by format rather than producing a single omni catalog may elect to use First Level.

3. The nature of materials being added to the collection. Locally produced or published materials are not likely to be listed in standard reference tools, nor found on the shelves of every library. Such material should be described in detail, for the cataloging record may be the only record of that item in existence. These items, as well as rare or valuable materials, should be cataloged at Level Two or Level Three. The chart in Figure 4-4 offers suggestions for deciding levels of description.

After the level of description has been selected the cataloger identifies and records the desired elements found in the technical reading. Most of these elements are given in the Chief Source of Information. When giving a book a technical reading, examine the verso of the title page carefully for edition statements, copyright dates and other essential information. Nonbook materials need equally careful treatment in technical reading, since producers are more likely to spread details of the descriptive elements on various parts of the packaging.

Choosing the Appropriate Description Level

Since the mid-1970s CATALOGING IN PUBLICATION DATA (CIP) has been printed on the verso of the title page. CIP is an incomplete cataloging record supplied by the Library of Congress before a book is printed. It helps establish the main entry, identifies the title, and indicates notes. Always take note of this information during the technical reading.

Cataloging in Publication

Step Three. *Identify and record the descriptive elements.*

A title is essential at any level of description and catalogers have characterized and defined the various types.

> *Title Proper*—the chief name for a work, including an alternative title, but excluding other types of title information.

Title and Statement of Responsibility

Alternative Title — the second part of a title proper, consisting of two parts joined by "or."

The Tempest, or, The enchanted island

Marcel Marceau, ou, L'art du mime

Parallel Title — the title proper in another language. Parallel titles are preceded by the = sign.

To catch a mongoose = Pour attraper une mangouste

Other Title Information — A subtitle that further amplifies the meaning of the title proper. A colon preceded and followed by a space separates the title proper from other title information.

Africa : adventure in eyewitness history

Collective Title — A title proper that is an inclusive title for an item containing several works. Collective titles may be taken from any source of information. When

FIRST LEVEL	• Accept First Level description given in prepared cataloging copy purchased by the library. • When staffing is inadequate, use First Level for most cataloging produced in the library. • Consider using First Level for materials listed in common bibliographic tools. • Consider using First Level for materials included in common reference indexing tools. • Consider using First Level for fiction and juvenile titles requiring limited retrieval information: mysteries, romances, science fiction, and westerns.
SECOND LEVEL	• Accept Second Level description given in prepared cataloging copy purchased by the library. • Use at least Second Level for items of particular importance, e.g., a special collection of materials of local interest. • Use at least Second Level when it is important to include elements that distinguish one format from another, e.g., all versions of *Oliver Twist*.

THIRD LEVEL	• Always use Third Level when materials have a special local significance:
	    Locally published genealogies.
	    Locally produced materials added to the permanent collection.
	    Publications of local significance not likely to be included in standard bibliographic tools or reference sources.
	    Local oral histories.
	• Use Third Level for any rare or valuable item.

Figure 4-4

a collective title is used, the individual content titles may be listed in the notes area.

Pete Seeger's children's concert

Supplied Title — A brief descriptive title supplied by the cataloger when no title is found. Always enclosed in brackets [ ].

To record, transcribe the title proper exactly as it is worded, capitalizing only proper names. Some punctuation may be altered or replaced. Include apostrophes and commas as given. Record the periods used to denote initials or abbreviations, but omit the space that in normal usage follows a period to avoid confusing these with the full stops used in ISBD punctuation. A lengthy title may be shortened after the first five words, provided that no essential information is omitted. Indicate omissions with ellipses (. . .). When there is no given title, supply an appropriate one and enclose this in brackets.

ITEM	TITLE	SOURCE OF INFORMATION	TITLE PROPER AS RECORDED
book	F.B.I. in Peace and War	title page	F.B.I. in peace and war
film loop	Lettering for Projection	label on container	Lettering for projection
sound recording	Kindergarten Songs Kindergarten Album I	on jacket on label	Kindergarten album I
videotape	recorded seminar	cataloger	[Kevin Jones, Law Day, May 1, 1987]
book	Guidelines Regarding Individuals Responsible for Continued Professional Development Program for Teachers in Local Education Agencies	title page	Guidelines regarding individuals responsible for continued professional development . . .

Recording the General Material Designations

Use of the GMD, an option provided by AACR2, is recommended for those libraries that collect many types of materials and enter everything in an omni catalog. In order to alert the user to the general format of the item, place the GMD directly after title proper, separating it from other parts of the title. Only alternative titles are not affected. When this option is taken always select the GMD from the appropriate list (See Figure 4-1). Be consistent in both terminology and form.

Alternative title   Marcel Marceau, ou, L'art du mime [text]

Parallel title   To catch a mongoose = Pour attraper une mangouste

Subtitle	Africa {text} : adventure in eyewitness history
Supplied title	{Ali-Holmes heavyweight title fight, 1980} {videorecording}

Other Title Information

Subtitles may be omitted with First Level. However, they often provide a fuller explanation of the work and are especially important when the title proper is uninformative about the content. *Belly to belly, back to back,* for instance, is about "the militant humanism of Robert R. Carkhoff," as its subtitle indicates. Users will not recognize this work for what it is unless the subtitle is included.

To add subtitles or parallel titles to a First Level description, place them (with proper punctuation) either in the first paragraph, or first in the notes area.

Second and Third Level description contain all title information. Note that Other Title Information is preceded by a space, colon, space (:). Parallel titles are distinguished by the equal sign (=).

First Level	Belly to belly, back to back /
Notes for First Level	Subtitle: The militant humanism of Robert R. Carkhoff
Second Level	Belly to belly, back to back {text} : the militant humanism of Robert R. Carkhoff /

Statements of Responsibility

The Chief Source of Information normally indicates who wrote, sang, illustrated, or otherwise participated in the item's creation. This information, the statement of responsibility, is transcribed immediately after the title information and separated from it by a slash. First Level suggests recording such a statement only when it differs from the main entry. Second Level includes all prominent names, while Third Level lists all those responsible for the work. List these names in the order in which they appear, taking the form of the name as given, but omitting titles unless they are an integral part of the name (e.g., Dr. Seuss). Transcribe exactly as given in the Chief Source of Information, including words describing participation, such as illustrated, edited, or written. If no such words appear they should not be added unless absolutely necessary for clarity, in which case enclose them in brackets, e.g., {drawings by}. If four or more people perform the same function (e.g., author) omit all but the first person listed. Explanatory notes or phrases may be added if the relationship between the work and the person is not clear. Do not construct a statement of responsibility if none appears prominently in the item.

Chief Source of Information (Title Page)	Dive! the Story of an Atomic Submarine Commander H. B. Harris-Warren, U.S.N.
First Level	Dive! [text]
Second Level	Dive! [text] : the story of an atomic submarine / H. B. Harris-Warren. — New York

Chief Source of Information (Record label)	The fall of the House of Usher and other tales by Edgar Allan Poe read by Vincent Price.
First Level	The fall of the House of Usher [sound recording]
Second Level	The fall of the House of Usher [sound recording] : and other tales / by Edgar Allan Poe; read by Vincent Price. —

Chief Source of Information (Title page)	Teaching Mathematics, Psychological Foundations F. Joe Crosswhite John L. Higgins Alan R. Osborne Richard J. Shumway
First Level	Teaching mathematics / F. Joe Crosswhite . . . [et al.]. —
Second Level	Teaching mathematics [text] : psychological foundations / F. Joe Crosswhite . . . [et al.]. —

An edition consists of all copies of an item produced from the master copy. Subsequent editions may make substantial changes in the original content; thus, catalogers treat editions as distinct works. When edition information is found in the Chief Source of Information, it is recorded following the statement of responsibility. Use standard abbreviations (see appendix) and arabic numbers in place of words; i.e., 3rd, not third. In Second and Third Levels also include any statements of responsibility related to a new edition, such as the editor who prepared the revision.

Edition Area

Chief Source of Information (Title page)	A Dictionary of Modern English Usage by H. W. Fowler Second Edition revised by Sir Ernest Gowers

First Level   A dictionary of modern English usage. — 2nd ed. —

Second Level   A dictionary of modern English usage / by H. W. Fowler. — 2nd ed. / rev. by Ernest Gowers. —

Publication, Distribution, etc.

The area of publication includes the names of all publishers, distributors, or agencies responsible for making the item available. For all levels, these names are listed in the order in which they appear in the Chief Source of Information. First Level omits place of publication; all levels include a publication or production date. Transcribe the name of the town or city as it appears, unless addition of a larger geographical unit aids identification (e.g., Garden City, N.J.). Use a space, colon, and space (:) between the place and the name of the agency, and abbreviate the name to the shortest form by which it can be recognized. Generalities such as "Company" or "Ltd." are entirely omitted. Use the most recent date given in the Chief Source of Information, unless there is a wide variance between publication and copyright dates. When this occurs, make it known by including both. For nonbook materials, it is always important to consult the Chief Source of Information for the original date of production. Many older copyrighted materials have been reissued and this is not always apparent on the new packaging. Supply an approximate date when no date is given and enclose this in brackets.

Chief Source of Information	*As recorded*
no date given, but probably produced in the 1970s	, [197-?]
McGraw-Hill Book Company	: McGraw-Hill,
The Oryx Press in Phoenix	. — Phoenix [Ariz.] : Oryx Press,
1979 publication date on the package, 1967 copyright date on the title frame	, 1979, c1967
Published by Western Publishing Company, New York. Developed by Academic Games Associates, Inc.	. — New York : Western Publishing : Developed by Academic Games Assoc., 1969. —

Those publishers who have offices in several cities usually list all of them. The cataloger need only name the first, e.g., R. R. Bowker

Company, New York and London. — New York : Bowker. If the first-named city is not in the home country of the cataloger, however, both can be recorded. A cataloger in England would record the above as: — New York ; London : Bowker.

For the physical description area the cataloger will rely on a technical reading to answer these four questions:

Physical
Description Area

> What is the extent of the item?
> What are its other physical details?
> What are its dimensions?
> Does it come with accompanying materials?

Formerly, users could assume that whatever physical details were supplied, they applied to the book. Now it is necessary to record descriptions of all available formats according to a prescribed method.

The GMD alerts users to the general form in which the content is packaged, such as a sound recording, but whether this sound recording is on cartridge, cassette, disk, or tape should also be noted. This specific indication of format is supplied in the Physical Description Area with the SPECIFIC MATERIAL DESIGNATION. Whereas inclusion of the GMD is optional, recording the specific material designation is obligatory. Figure 4-5 relates the list of [GMD] terms to the more specific terms used in this area. These terms are used exclusively because formats and the terms used to describe them have proliferated. For example, Library of Congress has been cataloging "phonorecords" for years, while others have cataloged "sound discs" or "audio recordings." Terminology has even varied within catalogs.

Begin a new paragraph and record the extent of the item, using arabic numerals, standard terminology taken from the chart, and standard abbreviations (see appendix). For First Level, only the extent of the item need be recorded. Second and Third Levels require more extensive detail:

> Specific material designation (if other than a book)
> Size in number of pages, volumes, frames, length, or other suitable
>   unit of measure
> Presence of illustrations, use of color, dimensions, diameter, playing
>   speed, etc.
> Accompanying materials

The extent of the item is separated from other details by a space, colon, space (:), and accompanying material should be indicated with a plus sign (+). Figure 4-6 illustrates First and Second Level physical description for the various formats. Note the punctuation and types of details included for each.

SPECIFIC MATERIAL DESCRIPTIONS

CLASS OF MATERIALS	GMD (List 2)	SPECIFIC MATERIAL DESIGNATIONS
Books, pamphlets, and printed sheets	Text	Number of pages or leaves in accordance with the terminology suggested by the volume.
Cartographic materials	Map Globe	atlas diagram globe map map section profile relief model remote-sensing image view
Manuscripts	Manuscript	Record sequences of leaves or pages.
Music	Music	score vocal score condensed score piano score close score chorus score miniature score part piano (violin, etc.) conductor part If none of the terms above is appropriate, use v. of music or p. of music or leaves of music. If a manuscript, precede the term by ms.
Sound recordings	Sound recording	sound cartridge sound tape reel sound cassette sound track film sound disc Use terms piano roll, organ roll, etc. as appropriate for rolls. If GMD is used, drop sound from all the above, except the last.
Motion pictures and videorecordings	Motion picture Videorecording	film cartridge videocartridge film cassette videocassette film loop videodisc film reel videoreel If GMD is used, drop film or video from all the above.

Figure 4-5

SPECIFIC MATERIAL DESCRIPTIONS (continued)

CLASS OF MATERIALS	GMD (List 2)	SPECIFIC MATERIAL DESIGNATIONS
Graphic materials	Art original	art original
	Art reproduction	art print
	Chart	art reproduction
	Filmstrip	chart
	Flash card	filmslip
	Picture	filmstrip
	Slide	flash card
	Technical drawing	flip chart
	Transparency	photograph
		picture
		postcard
		poster
		radiograph
		slide
		stereograph
		study print
		technical drawing
		transparency
		wall chart
		Add to filmstrip and stereograph the words cartridge or reel as appropriate.
Computer files	Computer file	computer cartridge
		computer cassette
		computer disk
		computer reel
		As new physical carriers are developed, for which none of these terms is appropriate, give the name of the physical carrier qualified by the word computer, e.g., computer card.

Figure 4-5 (continued)

43

SPECIFIC MATERIAL DESCRIPTIONS (continued)

CLASS OF MATERIALS	GMD (List 2)	SPECIFIC MATERIAL DESIGNATIONS	
Artifacts and realia	Art original	art original	game
	Art reproduction	art reproduction	microscope slide
	Diorama	braille cassette	mock-up
	Game	diorama	model
	Microscope slide	exhibit	
	Model		
	Realia	If none of these terms is appropriate, give the name	
	Toy	of the item concisely (e.g., hand puppet, quilt, etc.).	
Microforms	Microform	aperture card	microfilm
		microfiche	micro-opaque
		If the GMD is used, drop the prefix micro for these terms.	
		Add cartridge, cassette, or reel as appropriate.	
Serials	no GMD	Give the relevant specific material designation for the class	
		of material to which the item belongs, (e.g., wall chart,	
		filmstrip, v., microfiche, etc.).	

Figure 4-5 (continued)

EXAMPLES OF FIRST AND SECOND LEVEL PHYSICAL DESCRIPTIONS

	FIRST LEVEL	SECOND LEVEL
Books	231p. (last arabic numbered page is 231) 3v. (the book is in three volumes)	231p. : ill., charts, 13 cm. 3v. : ports., 17 cm. Use ill. for all illustrated materials. If the book also contains charts, coats of arms, facsimiles, forms, genealogical tables, maps, music, plans, portraits, samples, indicate with term or its abbreviation.
Sound recordings	1 sound disc 2 sound cassettes	1 sound disc (30 min.) : $33\text{-}\frac{1}{3}$ rpm, stereo. ; 12 in. 2 sound cassettes (80 min.) : $3\frac{3}{4}$ ips, stereo The physical description is provided for the user's information. For example, it is likely the user will want to know how long a sound recording plays, at what speed, number of sound channels, and if there is accompanying material.
Motion pictures and videorecordings	1 film cassette 1 video cassette	1 film cassette (25 min.) : sd., b&w ; 16mm. 1 videocassette (38 min.) : sd., col.
Artifacts and realia	1 game 1 metric ruler	1 game : (board, cards, 6 tokens, 2 dice) + instructions 1 metric ruler : in box $25 \times 8 \times 3$ cm. + manual
Filmstrips	1 filmstrip 4 filmstrips	1 filmstrip (24 fr.) : sd., col. ; 35 mm. 4 filmstrips (40 fr. each) : sd., col ; 35 mm. 2 sound cassettes + 1 instructional guide
Slides	12 slides	12 slides : col. + 1 teacher's manual

Figure 4-6

Series Area   A series title is a collective title applied to a group of separate items, each of which has its own title. Although series information has nothing to do with physical description, it immediately follows this area, in the same paragraph. Series details are enclosed in parentheses, recorded and punctuated in the same manner as the title proper.

Series are usually PUBLISHER SERIES, that is, a publisher commissioned a number of authors to write individual works under a collective title. Examples include the *Rivers of America* series, the *I Can Read* series, and *The American Poets* series of filmstrips. More rare are AUTHOR SERIES, in which all the titles are written by the same person, as in *The Story of Civilization* by Will and Ariel Durant. Some materials are better known by their series name than by individual titles, and this is particularly true of educational materials, such as textbook series.

Although First Level omits series information entirely, libraries that choose this level of description may wish to include series information and provide access points for a series title familiar to users. This decision should be based on the anticipated needs of those who are likely to use the item being cataloged.

When using Second Level, record series information in full, providing statements of responsibility for a series editor, and include the ISSN number when given. Numbering within the series is recorded with standard abbreviations and arabic numerals.

> Family library of great music
> Harvard East Asian series ; 79
> Olympia Press traveller's companion series ; no. 105
> The Pocketbook library of great art

If series information is not clearly identified as such, omit it.

Notes Area   Not all catalog records contain notes. Typed and computerized records often omit them. Notes, however, provide information that is not easily given elsewhere. AACR2 describes 21 varieties of notes from which the cataloger can choose. Common types of notes include: page numbers of bibliographies; information about other editions of the work; lists of accompanying materials; intended audience or reading levels; a summary or list of contents; and other formats in which the content appears. For instance, school media centers may choose to include reading levels in the notes area. Annotations are often given for juvenile works, or for materials that are not easily browsed. For a COLLECTIVE WORK, such as a sound recording of folk tales or a book of plays, listing the individual titles may be important. Any unusual details of binding, title, or edition that may confuse the patron may be recorded in this area.

The notes area begins a new paragraph. List each in the same order as the descriptive elements, with notes about the title first and the series last. Notes can be added to any level of description, but are never obligatory and should be added judiciously. Some libraries may find it simpler to catalog at Level One, and supply descriptive details (such as a subtitle) in the notes as needed. Notes provide useful information, but also add to the expense of producing the record.

International Standard Book Numbers and the International Standard Serial Numbers (ISBN and ISSN) are numbers uniquely assigned to almost every book and series published. Some books have both an ISBN and an ISSN. These numbers are often noted in publishers' catalogs and advertisements and used in ordering. Place the ISSN with the series parentheses and the ISBN above the tracings. Use any standard numbers found on the materials when cataloging, even for First Level description. No special punctuation is required. — Standard Numbers

TERMS OF AVAILABILITY, the price of the item, is not recommended for inclusion in the public catalog. Many libraries do, however, record the cost of items in the shelf list in order to assess fines for damaged or lost materials. — Terms of Availability

Entries for most library materials can be made by using these general rules. Cartographic items, serials, and complex multimedia sets are considered later.

SUMMARY

Descriptive cataloging ensures that the catalog identifies and describes each item in the collection. Without catalog descriptions, users would be forced to examine the items themselves in order to use the collection. The requirements for details of description (Figure 4-7) vary from library to library because researchers, gothic romance enthusiasts, elementary school students, and business people have different information needs.

Collections that house all formats and have a single catalog should supply details that are not essential for a one-format catalog. The cataloger who must type each card will describe items less fully than one who can purchase prepared copy. Whereas AACR2 provides guidelines for describing all formats, the cataloger must decide on the level of description and the use of other options, such as the GMD.

In other areas there is little room for individual choice. Because libraries may wish to share resources, the cataloger should, by relying on the correct source of information, record the required elements with standard terminology and abbreviations, with ISBD punctuation, and in proper order. In this way the catalog will be

ELEMENTS OF DESCRIPTION	MAJOR POINTS TO CONSIDER WHEN LAYING OUT THE DESCRIPTION
Title	Transcribe exactly as it appears
	Lengthy titles may be shortened
	Capitalize only proper names
	Include apostrophes and commas as given
	Construct a missing title and enclose it in brackets
GMD	Use this option according to local guidelines
	Select from the appropriate GMD list; terms should not vary
Parallel Titles and	Level One — Omit
Subtitles	Level Two — Transcribe exactly as given, using rules for title proper
Statements of Responsibility	Name only those prominently featured on the item
	Level One — Name only those first listed for any responsible function
	Level Two — Include all functions and those prominently named as responsible
Edition	Include in all levels
	Level Two — Include any statement of responsibility given
	Use arabic numerals and standard abbreviations
Publication Details	Level One — List first given publisher, producer, distributor, etc. and date
	Level Two — Add place to all publishers, producers, distributors, etc. as given
	Use the most recent date given
	Supply an approximate date for undated items; enclose in square brackets
Physical Details	Record the physical properties of the item, using standard material designations. Terms should not vary
	Use arabic numerals and standard abbreviations
	Level One — Include only extent of item
	Level Two — Include additional physical details, such as dimensions, time, speed, size of film, etc.
Series	Level One — Omit
	Level Two — Transcribe series title as it appears, using rules for title proper
	Include statement of responsibility and ISSN when given
Notes	Create as appropriate
Standard Number	Include in all levels when available

Figure 4-7

capable of fulfilling not only today's information needs, but also those of the future.

CHAPTER REVIEW

Terms to understand:

alternative title	parallel title
author series	specific material designations
cataloging in publication (CIP)	publisher series
Chief Source of Information	standard terminology
collective title	supplied title
collective work	technical reading
elements of description	terms of availability
general material designations	title proper
levels of description	verso
other title information	

Descriptive cataloging:

Eight elements of description.
Punctuated with machine-readable punctuation (ISBD).
Chosen from the sources of information.
Described with one of three levels of description using standard terminology.

The process of constructing an entry:

Before identifying and recording the descriptive elements, determine format, source of information, and level of description by technical reading.

CHAPTER 5

DESIGNING THE DESCRIPTION

IT SHOULD be possible for a library patron to discover from a catalog entry whether or not an item is needed without consulting the item itself. This means the cataloger must take care when deciding what information is to be transcribed in that entry. Guidelines for identification of Chief Sources of Information, for standard rules of description, and for the process of technical reading, would seem to assure the production of standard records, but this is frequently not the case. An examination of two catalogs will show that two catalogers following the same rules often produce different descriptions. Catalogers often face items with no identifiable chief source, with bibliographic information spread across many areas of a complex audio-visual kit, or even title pages that record information in topsy-turvy fashion, disguising the names of author or publisher. Catalogers faced with such problems, and with different kinds of patrons to serve, will not always make the same decision.

First Level description is always a minimum requirement, but Chief Sources of Information frequently offer a great deal more than is required at this level. The physical description area in particular suggests many possibilities. Catalogers make different decisions that depend on their thought processes, the needs of the library, and their attachment to detail.

WHEN FIRST LEVEL IS NOT ENOUGH

It is recommended that librarians who must do original cataloging describe items at First Level whenever appropriate. For materials that would otherwise go uncataloged, or for such materials as popular fiction, First Level provides a standard description. However, First Level cannot always meet the needs of library users. For designers of instructional multimedia units the EXTENT OF THE ITEM is not enough; OTHER PHYSICAL DETAILS such as length, sound, or speed are essential. Library users searching for materials produced by a professional association may not be able to find them without full descriptions because these materials are often produced by one agency, published by another, and distributed by a third. Items produced by organizations for internal use have their own problems: there is no prepared copy, and they rarely follow standard formatting, or identify chief sources. At a time when information is available in a variety of formats, and serves a variety of specific needs, the cataloger will encounter many situations in which First Level is not enough.

PHYSICAL DESCRIPTION

The physical description area of a cataloging record is one of the most difficult to standardize. An examination of the physical item itself, not a Chief Source, furnishes most of the details. It is not easy, even for catalogers, to agree on what physical details are most important for such items as graphic materials or realia. First Level avoids such complications by simply recording the extent of the item using the Specific Material Designation (see Figure 4-5). For example:

1   sound cassette
2   videocassettes
1   globe

But sometimes, in order to produce a useful description, other physical details must be supplied, standardized as much as possible according to AACR2.

For anyone planning to use an item for programming, or in the classroom, the playing time, or the number of components in an item, is obviously important. Record this information in parentheses immediately after the extent of the item:

1   film strip (50 frames)
10   sound cassettes (60 min. each), or 10 sound cassettes (10 hrs.)
1   videocassette (1 hr., 30 min.)

Introduce other physical details by space, colon, space. Each subsequent detail is preceded by a comma. Dimensions follow, preceded by space, semicolon, space. Remember, when cataloging, punctuation comes before, not after, an element.

Each format identified in AACR2 has its own standard list of other physical details (see Figure 4-6, Second Level) to be added as needed, in prescribed order, to the Specific Material Designation. Some of these are too technical, or too rarely encountered, to be utilized in most libraries. Others are more basic. The following are examples of some common and useful other physical details that can be used with several formats. Use only those necessary, and study the order in which they are listed. Playing speed precedes number of sound channels, followed by sound, characteristics, and colors:

playing speed

1   sound disc (40 min.) : 33⅓ rpm.
1   sound cassette (60 min.) : 1¼ ips.

number of sound channels

1   sound disc (45 min.) : stereo.
1   sound cassette (30 min.) : mono.

sound characteristics

1   videocassette (30 min.) : sd.
1   film loop (4 min.) : si.

color

1   filmstrip (82 frames) : b&w.
3   posters : red and white
1   computer disk : col.

medium

1   art original : oil on canvas
2   art prints : engraving

negative

1   microfilm reel : negative
6   photographs : negative

When necessary, record dimensions. Add these after other physical details. Precede by space, semicolon, space.

dimension

1   videocassette (21 min.) : stereo, col. ; ½ in.
2   computer disks : sd., col. ; 5¼ in.

ACCOMPANYING MATERIALS

Defined as "materials issued with, and intended to be used with, the item being cataloged" ACCOMPANYING MATERIALS can take almost any format: answer sheets, slides, cassettes, pictures, instructions. No matter what the level of description, identify accompanying materials. The simplest way is to indicate them after the extent of the item, or other physical details (if noted), with a plus sign:

1 filmstrip + 1 sound cassette.
10 posters + 1 pamphlet.
285 pages + 20 slides + 1 manual.

But there are other ways of noting accompanying materials.

Separate Entry. If an item is to circulate alone, rather than with another, supply a separate catalog description. In the strict sense of the term the item is no longer accompanying material.

Multilevel Description. This provides for complete identification, in one record, of all parts that share a common bibliographic entry; and is used by national bibiliographic and other cataloging agencies. These descriptions can become lengthy, difficult to decipher, and complicated to create.

Notes. Minor accompanying, or supplementary, materials can be listed in the notes area, such as,

> Set includes teacher's manual.
> Comes with backup copy.
> With black-lined masters.

Sometimes simple acknowledgment of the presence of accompanying material is not sufficient; users still need to know the length of a videocassette, or the number of frames in a film strip, no matter what its status within an item. Accompanying material is described the same way as the predominant component.

> 235 p. : ill., col. + 1 videocassette
> (30 min.) : sd., col. ; ½ in.

Physical description areas vary widely from cataloger to cataloger. Record those details useful to immediate users, while resisting the temptation to produce long, detailed, and time-consuming descriptions.

MAKING CHOICES—NAMING NAMES

Chief Sources of Information are often crowded with names: distributors, editors, producers, conductors, narrators, and others. It is possible to ignore most of these, recording only a first statement of responsibility and a first publisher. It is also correct to list, in order, all those names that appear in their appropriate areas. Sometimes neither approach serves the user.

List names important enough to be traced in the statement of responsibility so as to provide an access point. For example, someone might well wish to retrieve all works conducted by Leonard Bernstein, or all plays starring Sir Laurence Olivier. Also list names that might influence a person's choice of an item, such as an illustrator. List names of local significance, but do not list names for those who have vague, undefined roles, even though their names appear on the chief source; for example, consultant, project director, advisor.

Today, information is not only published, but also distributed, released, and issued. These names also appear in the Chief Source and require still more decisions. Such names, however, usually mean little to a user selecting an item; indicating first publisher is usually adequate.

Normally the cataloger can depend on the sequence and layout of the Chief Source in deciding what is placed where in the composition of the statement of responsibility and the publication, distribution, etc. area. But sometimes they are too ambiguous to be of much help. When it is difficult to determine exactly who had what to do with an item—for example, which names should be listed in the statement of responsibility and which in the publication, distribution, etc. area—decide what seems to make the most sense. Some statements that do not clearly belong in either place, yet are important enough to be included, can be given in a note. For example, the title *Free to be . . . you and me* listed directly over the publisher name is followed by the statement "Project of the MS. Foundation." This statement could influence a user's choice, but does not seem to fit either area. Record it in a note.

A variety of descriptions can also result from confusion about choice of the Chief Source of Information. It is simple to identify a single title page, or a title or frame of a film strip, but what of a text book series with a different title page for each grade level? Or five different formats packaged in one box, each bearing a unique label? When there is no clear choice for Chief Source, either regard all the different sources as one, picking the one with the latest date; or, in the case of multi-part materials, pick the chief source of the predominant component.

Despite the need to standardize, individual libraries are free to decide whether to catalog and circulate an item separately or as part of a kit, whether to list other physical details important to local users while omitting the rest, and what to add in the notes area. Creating standard descriptions for nonstandard items also requires decisions. Catalogers rely on individual judgment as they follow the technical processes that produce a descriptive record.

THE PROCESS—FROM ITEM TO RECORD

The technical reading of most published materials is relatively simple, a matter of selecting the basic elements of description from an obvious Chief Source and recording them in the prescribed form.

Information from title page.

THE FIRST LADIES
by Margaret Brown Klaplthor

published by the White House Historical
Association with the cooperation of the National
Geographical Society, Washington D.C.

The title page of this book is actually two pages; a large two-page illustration occupies most of the space, restricting the amount left for bibliographic information. However, the author and title are immediately apparent. Only one problem is posed by the title page: what information to record in the publication, distribution, etc. area? Since the catalog record should reflect the Chief Source of Information as accurately as possible, the statement was recorded exactly as found.

The verso of a title page is considered a part of the Chief Source, and cataloging information is frequently recorded there. For example, this verso contains the date of publication, 1981; the edition, third; the LC card number, 81-5206, and the ISBN, 0-912308-14-1. These bits of information will be added to the record.

The physical description area cannot be completed without examining the book itself. A glance at the back of the book shows that 89 is the last numbered page, so this is recorded in the physical description area.

An examination of the text reveals that a colored portrait of each First Lady is an important part of the book, and this also is noted:

```
Klaplthor, Margaret Brown.
    The First Ladies. — 3rd. ed. —
Washington, D.C. : White House Historical
Association with the cooperation of the
National Geographical Society, 1981.
    89 p.  :  ill., ports.
```

Non-print materials are not usually so helpful to the cataloger. In the example below there is only this label on the videocassette:

No title frame appears when the item is played, but the first frame does indicate a copyright date of 1984 held by The Master Teacher. The title is accepted from the label and becomes the main entry. The Master Teacher is named in the publication, distribution, etc. area along with the copyright date. Physical details, including length, are determined by viewing the tape, and a series title is included. The paucity of information results in a First Level description:

```
Teaching word problem solving and
   mathematical insights [videorecording].
   -- Master Teacher, 1984.
   1 cassette (20 min.) : sd., col. ;
½ in. (The Master Teacher video series)
```

Sometimes, instead of having too little information, the cataloger is faced with too much. Multimedia kits often present several problems, especially when cataloged and circulated as one item. The following example, a drug education kit, has several distinct formats, each produced by a different entity in a different year. It circulated as one item.

The kit contains four items: a videocassette, a sound cassette, a computer disk, and an activity folder. The outside cover of the kit bears this information:

The back cover of the kit notes: "TEXIZE Greenville, S.C. 29602. Division of Dow Consumer Products, Inc. © 1987." The back cover also has this label:

> The National Crime Prevention Council, the U.S. Department of Justice (Bureau of Justice Assistance, Office of Justice Programs) and the Texize Division of Dow Consumer Products Inc. have developed this kit and brought it to you at no charge.

Turning to the individual components of the kit, the sound cassette bears this information:

> **McGruff's Drug Prevention and Child Protection Program**
> In cooperation with
> The National Crime Prevention Council
> and
> The Advertising Council
> © **1984, 1986 National McGruff Campaign**
> **P.O. Box 85266, San Diego, CA 92138**

This label appears on the computer disk:

The videocassette is housed in a plastic container that bears this label:

And the outside of the activity folder has this label:

This Kit Contains:

McGruff's "The No Show" videotape, a 23-minute fun yet meaningful presentation about kids having positive experiences without drugs

"The No Show" viewers' guide, which summarizes the plot of the video and offers discussion questions for kids and adults

The McGruff "No Show" Computer Game, a challenging exercise which reinforces McGruff's lessons

The McGruff Smart Kids Audio Cassette, packed with eleven anti-drug songs which kids can listen to and sing along with

Inside This Wrapper, Camera-Ready Masters For . . .

Kids
- "Winners Don't Use Drugs" brochure
- Seek & Find
- Secret Message
- Maze
- Finger Puppets
- Reproducible version of "The No Show" poster
- Answer sheet for all of the games

Parents
- Sample letter from McGruff describing the program
- "Talking With Your Kids About Drugs" flier

Also . . .

A list of educational materials for kids, available from the National Crime Prevention Council

A resource list, which includes national groups and federal agencies which can provide information on drug abuse prevention

Since each item has its own Chief Source of Information, a careful technical reading is necessary. The outside label and the activities folder supply the only unifying information. The outside label provides the collective title "Drug Abuse Prevention Kit," which becomes the main entry. The outside label also contributes information for the publication, distribution, etc. area. The activities folder lists the three agencies that developed the kit and these can be added in the statement of responsibility, completing the body of the card. Though "Project Kids Care" appears on several items, its role is undefined; it will be mentioned in a note.

The physical description area is next. Since no item predominates it is possible to transcribe "1 Kit." Other options include listing the extent of each item, ending with the words "in container"; or providing a separate physical description for each on a separate line. The assumed use of the kit should determine the choice. Since this kit was produced for those designing programs about drugs it is decided that other physical details should be noted for each item.

The notes must now be composed. "Project Kids Care" is listed since it appeared so prominently. Computer system requirement is an essential note and is recorded. McGruff is a nationally known symbol for crime prevention so is also added as a content note.

A detailed cataloging description has been designed based on the projected use of this kit:

```
Drug abuse prevention kit / developed by the National
    Crime Prevention Council, U.S. Dept. of Justice,
    and Texize. -- Greenville, S.C. : Texize, 1987.
1 videocassette (23 min.): sd., col.; ½ in.
1 computer disk : sd., col.; 5¼ in.
1 activity folder.
In container 33 × 26 × 5 cm.

''Project Kids-Care'' on container.
McGruff's Child Protection and Drug Prevention Program.
Computer disk system requirements: Apple II, IIe or IIc.
```

UNPUBLISHED ITEMS

Perhaps the most difficult types of items to catalog are those produced locally and considered UNPUBLISHED ITEMS by AACR2. Oral histories, inhouse videos, locally printed biographies can be lost or forgotten if uncataloged. Since standard copy is not available, these items require original cataloging. Often unique to the collection, they demand full description, but there is often little bibliographic information to aid the cataloger.

The following example is a videocassette with no label, merely a penciled note, "Jupiter History." To discover more about this video it is necessary to view it and take notes, pausing whenever a bibliographic detail occurs. The producer provides title frames, and includes a statement of responsibility. No dates are given, although it is possible to discover a date from an introductory statement made early in the video. Viewing the video reveals two separate programs: an interview with three pioneers from Jupiter, Florida, and a presentation about the history of the Jupiter Lighthouse.

The first decision is about the title. Is it better to supply a collective title such as Jupiter Florida History, or record the two individual programs? The cataloger chooses to accept the two titles as listed in the title frame and transcribe them according to the rules in AACR2. The statement of responsibility is taken directly from the title screen. Since the item falls under the rules of unpublished materials, adding other information, beyond a date, is unnecessary.

The note area is full. Since this is an original item it is not described in standard bibliographical terms. This may well be the only, or one of a few, descriptions extant. Since it cannot be browsed, it requires more information than other items, including a summary of the content:

```
    Pioneers of the Jupiter area : the Jupiter
       Lighthouse [videorecording] / Loxahatchee
       Historical Society and Jupiter Elementary
       School. -- 1987.
       1 cassette (ca. 60 min.) :  sd.,  col.  ; ½ in.
       Produced by JoAnn Ritter's 5th grade class.
    Narrated by Jack Needs, Principal.
       Summary: Two oral histories interviewing
    Jupiter, FL. pioneers Anna Minear, Wilhelmina
    Bennett, Bessie Dubois, and lighthouse keeper
    Jack Oakland.
```

SUMMARY

When doing original cataloging, first consider describing the item at First Level. Sometimes the needs of the users make this inappropriate. This is especially true of multimedia kits, unpublished materials, and non-standard packaging. The cataloger makes a series of individual decisions when cataloging these materials, based as closely as possible on the standards provided by AACR2. Use common sense and avoid excessive detail.

CHAPTER REVIEW

Terms to understand:
  accompanying materials
  extent of the item

multilevel description
notes
other physical details
separate entry
unpublished items

Other physical details:

Are added to the physical description area in prescribed order as needed to help the user select from the catalog.

Accompanying materials:

Must always be indicated. Describe by the same criteria used for the item they accompany.

CHAPTER 6

PROVIDING ACCESS POINTS: AACR2, PART II

A RECORD must have headings so that it can be found in the catalog. The cataloger assigns these access points after completing the description. When standardized, they gather together items with common bibliographic features, allowing the catalog to show how many works by Jane Austen, or which editions of *Alice in Wonderland*, are available. So the second purpose of the catalog, that of organizing the collection bibliographically, is achieved. Part II of AACR2 is the basic tool for choosing and recording headings.

MAIN ENTRY

The concept of a main entry, a primary access point assigned to each item, is not as valid as it used to be. When cataloging information is retrieved by a computer, main and added entries are equally important because the descriptive record can be retrieved from any assigned access point. Indeed, even with the unit card system, in which the cataloger added access points to cards that were otherwise identical, both main and added entries led to complete information. Nonetheless, it is useful to have one standard access point, universally agreed upon, which will always identify a certain item.

Standardized entries make it easier to share materials with other libraries, so the rules in AACR2 should be carefully followed. In reality, catalogers have limited choice, because main and added entries are nearly always selected from bibliographic details found in the Chief Source of Information. Normally, the main entry is an author, a title, or a corporate body. Authors have always been first choice for main entry (at least in the Western world), and when there is a single person obviously responsible for the work, that name is chosen. If more than one person is involved, the principal author or the first name listed is selected.

When the term author was defined during the 19th century for the purposes of cataloging, the definition was expanded to include not only editors and compilers, but corporate bodies as well. This interpretation led to a number of complex problems in this century as corporations and government agencies multiplied, divided, changed names, and extended their activities. As a result the average library user today has little chance of locating anything under a corporate name. AACR2 now restricts the circumstances for entering corporations as main entries and denies main entry to editors and compilers. Under this code, the name of a corporate body can only be a main entry when the item is definitely a statement about the corporation's internal operations and activities.

Title main entry is assigned when a work has four or more authors; when the author is unknown or cannot be determined; when only an editor or compiler is named; when the work is issued by a corporate body, has no author, but does not fit a category for corporate entry; or is regarded as sacred scripture.

Access points can also be assigned to other names listed on the title page such as joint authors, editors, or compilers. These added entries provide additional access points.

These simple guidelines will solve most problems of choosing main entries; however, after they are chosen they must be recorded in a standard manner. Even when taken from the Chief Source of Information, questions about their correct form may persist. For instance, authors write under different names and in unfamiliar languages, corporate structure may be difficult to understand, and sacred scripture follows special rules. AACR2 provides guidance for recording access points consistently.

A personal author is an individual chiefly responsible for the content of a work. Operas, plays, games, sonatas, novels, textbooks, and paintings can all be works of personal authorship and cataloged under single, principal, or first-named authors who are easily identified from the Chief Source of Information. When a work is one of SHARED RESPONSIBILITY, that is, created by two or more people, the principal author (the name that appears most prominently) is the main entry. If no single name stands out, select the first-named author and include the other names as added entries.

Personal Names as Entries

It is not so simple to identify the principal authors of works of MIXED RESPONSIBILITY such as revisions, adaptations, or books containing text and illustrations by different people. For example, what is the correct procedure for cataloging a journalist's interview with a member of the government, or a recording of a performer's adaptation of a composer's score?

Such works fall into two broadly defined categories: modifications of previously published materials, and collaborations producing new works when the contributions have been of different kinds. A modification of a work is entered under the new author if there have been substantial changes in the content of the work or its medium. If the modification is merely an updating, rearrangement, or abridgment, enter under the original author. The deciding factor is the amount of the original work that remains. When *Hamlet* is transferred verbatim to a sound recording it is still *Hamlet* and is entered under Shakespeare. *Hamlet* as retold for children by Charles and Mary Lamb is entered under Lamb. The musical *My Fair Lady* retains some of the language of George Bernard Shaw's play *Pygmalion*, but for the most part was written and composed by Alan Jay Lerner and Frederick Loewe, who get the credit in the catalog. The cataloger is not obliged to read editions or compare films with texts to determine content change. Accept whatever is listed in the Chief Source of Information, preferring the original author's name when that has been retained. Children's librarians who prefer to have all adaptations, revisions, and simplified versions under the original author can achieve this by providing an added entry for that person.

Loewe, Frederick, 1904–
    My fair lady / music by Frederick Loewe ; book and lyrics by Alan Jay Lerner ; adapted from Bernard Shaw's Pygmalion.

Efron, Marshall.
    Bible stories you can't forget, no matter how hard you try / Marshall Efron & Alfa-Betty Olsen ; illustrated by Ron Barrett.

Another kind of decision is made when an item has been created by several people with different responsibilities. Examples include children's picture books with both authors and illustrators; autobiographies written in collaboration with professional writers; and the letters of famous people selected and edited by others. In these cases the cataloger must decide whether the work is a collaboration and, if so, enter it as an item with joint authors. Then the main entry will be the principal, or first-named author, and the statement of responsibility will follow the Chief Source of Information. If, on the basis of the Chief Source, the cataloger judges it the work of one author and not a collaboration, it should be entered as such.

Ginsburg, Mirra.
    The chick and the duckling / translated and adapted from the Russian of V. Suteyev ; pictures by Jose & Ariane Aruego.

Iacocca, Lee A.
    Iacocca, an autobiography / Lee Iacocca ; with William Noval.

Recording Personal Names

After the cataloger has selected a personal name as a main (or added) entry, that name is normally recorded in the form given in the Chief Source. Care must be taken, however, to ensure that works created by the same person are found together in the catalog. The cataloger is responsible for the record of an entire collection, and items in that collection should be gathered bibliographically. Unfortunately, personal names are not always recorded uniformly in Chief Sources of Information. Sometimes a full name will appear, sometimes initials or even nicknames. The rules call for entry under "the most frequently used name," whether it is a nickname, pseudonym, title of nobility, initials, or other appellation. This does not mean that the cataloger must do extensive research. When a personal name appears in the CIP data, accept it; otherwise record it as it appears in the Chief Source of Information. If the author's name appears in several forms the cataloger makes a decision, consulting reference sources if necessary.

Sometimes main entry differs from the statement of responsibility in the descriptive paragraph. Samuel Clemens wrote under the pseudonym Mark Twain. If the work is entered under his pseudonym, but gives his real name on the title page, the statement of responsibility differs, as in the following example.

Twain, Mark.
    A Connecticut Yankee in King Arthur's court / by Samuel Langhorne Clemens.

This procedure also applies to authors who occasionally record their initials on the title page, but have written other works under their full name.

Findlay, John Niemeyer.
    Kant and the transcendental object : a hermeneutic study / by J. N. Findlay.

Accept the Chief Source of Information for those people who publish under pseudonyms or change their names.

Carroll, Lewis, 1832–1898.
    Anderson's Alice : Walter Anderson illustrates Alice's adventures in wonderland / by Lewis Carroll ; with a foreword by Mary Anderson Pickard.

Eliot, George, 1819–1880.
    The mill on the floss / George Eliot ; edited by Gordon S. Haight.

It is not necessary to add dates of birth and death or biographical information. Only when several people with the same name appear in the catalog is it necessary to distinguish between them by adding information.

Burrell, Robert Michael.
    Iran, Afghanistan, Pakistan : tension and dilemmas / R. M. Burrell and Alvin J. Cottrell.
    (Joint authors. Name on title page, R. M. Burrell, but other works already entered under Robert Michael Burrell.)

Buchwald, Art.
    The Buchwald stops here / Art Buchwald.
(Commonly used nickname.)

Rossetti, Anton, 1746–1792.
Rossetti, Dante Gabriel, 1828–1882.
(Dates are used to help distinguish between two similar names.)

H. D. (Hilda Dolittle).
Lawrence, D. H. (David Herbert).
(Full name in parentheses added for identification.)

Even when relying on the Chief Source of Information, the cataloger may still have questions. Forenames should be used for royalty, saints, and members of religious orders, and clarified by a designation, or identifying phrase.

John, Abbot of Ford.
    Sermons on the Song of Songs / John of Ford ; translated by Wendy Mary Beckett

John XXIII, Pope
Benedict, Saint

For compound names, or names with prefixes, follow the form of the language in which the author writes. Hyphenated names are treated as a single word.

Ashton-Warner, Sylvia.
    I passed this way /

Du Maurier, Daphne
De la Mare, Walter
Lloyd George, David
Goethe, Johann Wolfgang von

Classical writers are entered under the names by which they are best known in English; e.g., Horace, Cicero, Virgil.

Homer.
    Homer's Iliad / translated, with an introduction by Denison Bingham Hull

Titles of nobility are used if the person is commonly known by that title and appears under it in reference sources.

Byron, George Gordon Byron, Baron, 1788–1824.
The complete poetical works / Lord Byron ; edited by
Jerome J. McGann

Few problems will arise if the name is recorded in the form
generally used by the author, or in the form given in the Chief
Source of Information. There will always be someone, however, who
searches for Stendhal under Beyle, Unamuno y Jugo under Jugo, or
Van Greenaway under Greenaway, and CROSS REFERENCES should
therefore be made from the name not used to the other, e.g.,

Clemens, Samuel Langhorne

see

Twain, Mark

La Mare, Walter de

see

De la Mare, Walter

Corporate Bodies as Entries

A corporate body is an organization or group that acts as a single
entity and is identified by a particular name. Examples include
associations, institutions, businesses, government agencies, religious bodies, churches, and conferences. The publications of corporate bodies are very numerous and cataloging them can be a
challenge.

The occasions when a corporate main entry is assigned are limited
by AACR2 to the following types of materials:

Items of an administrative nature that deal with the corporation
itself, such as newsletters, annual reports, regulations, rules, and mem-
bership lists.

Documents such as laws, treaties, decrees, court decisions, consti-
tutions, and legislative hearings.

Collective thought of a body, such as a statement issued by the
American Medical Association, or a committee report from the Parent-
Teacher Association.

Works that record the activities of a conference, such as the White
House Conference on Aging, or an academic symposium.

Works that are the products of established performing groups, such
as The Who, the Amadeus Quartet, and the New York Philharmonic,
when their responsibility goes beyond mere performance.

Cartographic materials that have some relationship to a corporate body other than simple publication.

If a work does not fit any of these categories, do not enter it under a corporate name even if a corporation paid for the publication and printed its name on it.

Examples of Corporate Entry:

Inter-American Development Bank.
   Agreement establishing the Inter-American Development Bank.

United States.
   Copyright law of the United States of America.

United States. Federal Home Loan Bank Board.
   Agenda for reform : a report on deposit insurance to Congress from the Federal Home Loan Bank Board / Richard T. Pratt, Jamie Jay Jackson

AMA Congress on Environmental Health Problems.
   Proceedings

Beatles.
   Past masters [sound recording] / The Beatles

Smithsonian Associates.
   Guide to the nation's capital and the Smithsonian Institution [map]

Although corporate publications are found in every collection, cataloging copy for them is rarely available. The public library can be expected to have directories of local agencies, manuals from local governments, and annual business reports; school libraries have college catalogs and illustrated catalogs from art galleries; college libraries house materials produced by conferences and symposiums; and church libraries collect reports from missions and records of conferences. These materials often constitute the bulk of special library collections. Although some of these materials may be left uncataloged, others should be added to the general collection, and the rules should therefore be understood.

Recording
Corporate Names

The basic rule for corporate bodies is the same as that for personal authors: enter under the name most likely to be known by the user. Entry under corporate body is more confusing than entry under person, because these bodies change their names frequently, names are hard to track down, and corporations often contain many subordinate agencies.

Under the present rules, when a corporate body changes names it becomes a new entity. If necessary, create a cross reference tying the names together. When a corporate body lists its name differently in the Chief Source of Information and in its various publications, select the name appearing in a more formal position (head of the title, statement of responsibility, etc.). If that doesn't work, decide which name is most common and choose its briefest form.

NATO Advanced Institute on Atoms in Unusual Situations (1985: Cargese, Corsica).
    Atoms in unusual situations /

AFL-CIO.
    The AFL-CIO platform proposals, presented to the Republican and Democratic national conventions, 1968

ERIC—not Educational Resources Information Center
OCLC—not Online Computer Library Center
UNESCO—not United Nations Educational Scientific & Cultural Organization

Libraries are cataloging more and more information in the form of reports from conferences, workshops, and symposiums. When the title of such a meeting appears in the Chief Source of Information, that name may be used as the main entry. Add the number of the conference, and the date and place in parentheses when known.

Conference
Reports

NATO Conference on the Acquisition of Symbolic Skills (1982: University of Keele).
    The acquisition of symbolic skills /

Entry under a corporate body presents one problem that entering under author does not: people do not have subdivisions, or subordinate and related bodies.

The general rule is to enter a subordinate name directly as a heading in the catalog when it is a distinctive name, appearing on a publication. Enter it as it appears. For example:

Air Pollution Technical Information Center

is a subordinate body, part of the Environmental Protection Agency. It does not depend on its parent body for identification, however, and is entered directly in the catalog as an independent unit:

> Air Pollution Technical Information Center.
> Air pollution technical publications of the U.S. Environmental Protection Agency.

In other cases, when a subheading is insufficient to identify the item in the catalog, it must be entered under its parent body. AACR2 identifies such subheadings as those including words indicating a relationship with a higher body (department or division), or implying administrative subordination (committee). Others may have names so general, or so removed from the idea of a corporation, they must be linked to their parent. Departments or units within a university or college, or names that are included in the entire name of a larger institution, also cannot stand alone.

> Institute of Medicine (U.S.). Division of Mental Health and Behavioral Medicine
>
> American Institute of Certified Public Accountants. Committee on Stockbrokerage Auditing
>
> Harvard University. Program on Technology and Society
>
> Georgia State University. Southern Labor Archives
>
> Harvard Law School. Library

Although the situation is more complicated when the unit issuing the work is the lowest link of an organization's hierarchy, the cataloger takes the same approach. If the entire hierarchy is listed it will be extremely long, so omit any part of the chain not needed to link the smaller body with the larger one. For example, United Nations, Department of International Economic and Social Affairs, Center for Social Development and Humanitarian Affairs is entered as:

> United Nations. Center for Social Development and Humanitarian Affairs

Since there is only one such center in the U.N. it will not lose its identity when entered directly under United Nations.

Government Agencies

As anyone who has searched through the United States entries of a catalog realizes, rules for corporate bodies also include agencies of the government. Partly because these entries were becoming so cumbersome, the principles of entry under government bodies were simplified by AACR2, and are now identical to those for non-government bodies. If the agency has a unique name, such as Library of Congress, that does not suggest dependent status, it is entered under its own name:

National Academy of Sciences (U.S.)

National Science Foundation

However, if the name of the subordinate unit implies that it is dependent, or if the name of the government is needed to identify the agency, enter it as a subordinate body.

California. Bureau of Educational Research.
  Evaluating pupil progress / Prepared by Henry Magnuson

United States. Commission on Civil Rights
Georgia. Judicial Planning Committee
New Hampshire. Office of State Planning

Not only are states, towns, and countries entered as corporate bodies, but also the official acts of the heads of these entities. The form is as follows: government, title with years of incumbency, brief form of person's name:

United States. President (1977–1981 : Carter).
  Public papers of the Presidents of the United States

United States. President (1961–1963 : Kennedy).
United Kingdom. Sovereign (1952–   : Elizabeth II).

This form is only for official publications. Material that does not fall into this category is entered in the same way as a personal author:

Carter, Jimmy, 1924–
  Keeping faith : memoirs of a president

Kennedy, John Fitzgerald.
  Profiles in courage

Geographic Names

It is often necessary for the cataloger to distinguish between corporate names or government bodies by adding geographic location. For instance, a First National Bank might exist in any hamlet and there is a Court of Appeals in every state. The general rule is to use the English form of the name as found in a gazetteer. When it is necessary to distinguish between places with the same name, add the name of the next-largest geographical unit.

Columbia Historical Society (Washington, D.C.).
  Records –– Columbia Historical Society of Washington, D.C.

71

New York (Colony).
An abridgment of the Indian affairs contained in four folio volumes

New York (N.Y.). Office of Management and Budget.
Adopted budget : as certified by the Mayor, the Comptroller, and the City Clerk

First National Bank (Springfield, Mo.)
First National Bank (Springfield, Ill.)

Titles as Entries

The title is such an important means of identifying an item that, when one cannot be found, it is invented by the cataloger, which is not true of other areas of description. Some catalogers argue that title makes a better choice than author for main entry, because there is only one title, whereas author main entry often presents a number of candidates. Certainly, nonbook materials are simpler to enter under title, as often there are several people involved in the performance of a piece of music or the creation of a film, and a principal author cannot easily be selected. AACR2 defines the concept of author very narrowly: editors and compilers are not considered authors; corporate bodies can only be authors under restricted rules. In these cases, as when the author is unknown, or when there are more than three authors, enter under title. Sacred scripture has long been entered under title.

Recording Titles

Simple title entry is not a problem. During the descriptive process the title is identified and recorded from the Chief Source of Information. When the title is selected as an entry, it is already constructed. But the second purpose of the catalog has still to be achieved.

Uniform Titles

The cataloger is responsible for bringing together different editions of the same work. These often have different individual titles, such as *Alice in Wonderland* and *Alice's Adventures in Wonderland*. When the same work has different titles in different editions, the cataloger selects a UNIFORM TITLE that brings them together in the catalog.

Catalogers have long had rules for using uniform titles for certain categories of works: sacred scripture (the Bible or Koran), laws and treaties, and anonymous classics (*Mother Goose*, *Beowulf*, and the *Arabian Nights*). The need for uniform titles has also been recognized when title is used for an added entry. *Hamlet*, for example, may have different titles in its various editions, but users will expect to find *Hamlet* under either Shakespeare or *Hamlet*, so a uniform title is used as the title access point. This is also called the FILING TITLE in some cataloging manuals.

Because sacred scripture exists in numerous editions, they are entered in the catalog under uniform titles. To the uniform title add language, version, and year:

Bible. English. Douay. 1910.

Selections are arranged thus:

Bible. N.T. Acts. English. Lattimore. 1982.
   Acts and Letters of the Apostles / newly translated from the Greek by Richmond Lattimore.

Bible. N.T. Gospels. English. Authorized. Selections. 1984.
   Christmas, the King James Version.

Anonymous classics are works that have been available since before 1500, have appeared under a variety of titles, and whose authors are unknown. In these cases uniform titles are used for the main entry regardless of variant editions.

Mother Goose.
   Mother Goose rhymes [game] /

Mother Goose.
   Brian Wildsmith's Mother Goose /

When a uniform title is used as main entry the hanging indention card format is not used. The card follows the format used for author main entry instead.

Beowulf.
   The Therekelin transcripts of Beowulf / translated by Kemp Malone.

Beowulf.
   Beowulf : a verse translation into modern English / by Edwin Morgan.

Like other adaptations, however, anonymous classics are entered under the name of the adapter when the text has been rewritten.

Hosford, Dorothy.
   By his own might : the battles of Beowulf / Dorothy Hosford ; drawings by Lasylo Matulay.

Williams, Jay.
   The horn of Roland / Jay Williams

No standard uniform titles have been created for works published since 1500, so when a work has appeared under varying titles the cataloger should select the best-known. Use the following forms:

Shakespeare, William.
   [Hamlet]
   The tragedy of Hamlet, the Prince of Denmark / by
William Shakespeare.

Musical works often have popular titles in addition to those given by their composers. Using music reference tools, the cataloger creates uniform titles to bring the works together.

Other situations also call for decisions about uniform titles. An abridgment may be published under a different title from the original edition; a book or film first released in England may bear a different title when issued in America; different editions of the same reference work or textbook series may have different titles. Uniform titles should be created according to the cataloger's expectation of users' needs and may vary from one catalog to another.

ADDED ENTRIES

After recording the main entry, the problem of selecting and recording added entries remains. The main reason to select additional access points is the judgment that someone may look for that item under that heading. Most libraries choose to make added entries according to their staffing resources and the needs of their users. Added entries can usually be found in the Chief Source of Information, but an added entry does not have to be made for every bibliographic detail listed there.

Added entries are normally made in the same form as main entries, but titles are sometimes traced differently. Occasionally there may be a need for access to a partial title, alternative title, or subtitle, and an additional title tracing will be provided. For example, the Golden Press published a great many titles for juveniles that start with "The Golden Book of": *The Golden Book of Facts and Figures*, *The Golden Book of Fun and Nonsense*, *The Golden Book of the Civil War*, *The Golden Book of the Renaissance*. Users may be inclined to search under Facts and Figures, especially if this phrase is printed in larger letters. It makes sense therefore to provide additional title access in the tracings:

1. Title II. Title: Facts and figures

CROSS REFERENCES

Because the cataloger can never be certain that users will seek information under the main and added entries that have been selected, SEE and SEE ALSO references are used. *See* guides the user from a name or term not used, or recorded in a different form, to the relevant entry. The card for "Leonardo," for example, may read: "*See* da Vinci, Leonardo." *See also* guides the user from a name or term that is used to another, related entry that will provide additional information. If a catalog conflict has been created by following different codes and an author's works are entered under two names (Twain, Mark and Clemens, Samuel Langhorne), *see also* references can guide the user from one to the other.

Unfortunately, in many libraries that have been buying copy for their catalogs, the cross reference structure seems to have fallen into disuse. It is far too easy to purchase catalog cards, file them away, and ignore other aspects of catalog maintenance that would make it a better tool for users. If department store catalogs and telephone books find it necessary to use these references, certainly the more complex library or media center catalog should offer such aids. The use of cross reference is a matter of judgment on the part of catalogers.

AUTHORITY FILES

Many decisions are involved in the process of selecting and recording entries. To ensure consistency libraries maintain AUTHORITY FILES to record these decisions. Authority files give the chosen form of entry with any cross references that have been used. When physically convenient, a library's catalog is the best authority for forms of headings; however, it does not record cross references. A separate record for cross references allows all traces of a name or title to be removed from the catalog when a work is withdrawn. Authority files are found in card files, in microform and in online catalogs and are becoming increasingly important as libraries share records through automation.

SUMMARY

Access points provide entry to the information stored in the catalog. Standardization of these access points is important if works are to be related and gathered together in the catalog according to their bibliographic features. If libraries are to share materials and information through networks, they must agree on standard ways to identify works.

Catalogers select a main entry for each work. When an author, or authors, are clearly responsible for the work, main entry is under the personal name. Under certain clearly defined circumstances works are entered under corporate names (which include government bodies). Other works, including those with compilers and editors, are entered under title.

If all the works of an author, and all editions and titles of a work, are to be located in the catalog, the forms of the entries must be standardized. Usually the form as found in the Chief Source of Information is adequate; when there is conflict, select the form in most common use. Classics and sacred scriptures frequently have many variant titles that are standardized by a uniform title.

Even when cataloging information is purchased, it is necessary to do original cataloging with corporate publications, as many of these may be of limited or local issue. By following the code these materials can be integrated with the catalog and the rest of the collection.

See and *see also* references are important as they guide users to correct or to additional headings.

CHAPTER REVIEW

Terms to understand:

author entry	mixed responsibility
authority files	*see also* reference
corporate entry	*see* reference
cross references	shared responsibility
filing title	uniform title

Catalog headings or access points:

Based on bibliographic details
Recorded according to AACR2
Include author, title, and corporate entries

Author entries:

May be under a personal author: the only, principal, or first-named author in the Chief Source of Information.
When responsibility for authorship is mixed, as in an adaptation or collaboration, follow the authority of the Chief Source to determine personal authorship.

Corporate entries:

Under circumstances defined by AACR2, works can be entered under the corporate name as found in the Chief Source of Information. Use brief forms, entering directly under the name of a subordinate body of an organization when that smaller body has a distinct identity. Otherwise enter under the largest body where it does not lose identity. If needed, identify the subordinate body by place.

Title entry:

Use a uniform title form for sacred scripture, anonymous classics, musical works, and variant titles.

Record the entries as found in the Chief Source of Information unless this causes conflict in the catalog.

In such cases, use the most common term.

Tie decisions together with cross references.

Record the decision in the authority file.

CHAPTER 7

ORGANIZING BY SUBJECT

USERS are often seeking not specific items that can be retrieved by an author or title heading, but materials dealing with particular subjects. Identification of the library's holdings by subject is therefore one of the catalog's most important functions. There is evidence that King Assurbanipal's librarians practiced a form of classification by shelving arrangement, and during the Middle Ages libraries were commonly arranged in this way rather than by author or title.

In order to identify library materials as individual items, or as part of a group, catalogers describe each work and provide standard access points. These are also the objectives of subject cataloging: to identify individual works whose subject is known, and to gather works on the same subject together. Although librarians have taken different approaches to the organization of knowledge, they have all struggled with the basic problem of how to relate materials to each other on the shelf, while relating them intellectually in the catalog.

FIXED VERSUS RELATIVE LOCATION

One of the oldest methods of gathering subjects on the shelf and in the catalog is FIXED LOCATION. In this arrangement all pamphlets are placed in chest A, and all books are stacked in chest B. Or all musical works are in the North Room and all art items in the South Room. They can be arranged by size, by order received, or in any other way that appeals to the cataloger. Today, collections on CLOSED SHELVES, which prohibit public access, are often shelved in fixed locations, usually to save space. In collections that cannot be browsed, such as a film library, fixed location is also a reasonable option. Library collections tend to grow, however, and someday the pamphlets will not fit into chest A, and a wing must be added to the South Room for the art works. Are there to be two art collections now, and then three and four? Or is a new scheme to be developed and the whole collection rearranged?

As a partial solution to the problem of growth, fixed collections can be arranged by accession number (order of purchase), which does allow new acquisitions to be added at one end. Film libraries often follow this scheme. Films are placed in strict numerical order by purchase, and a catalog provides access. Since film users will rarely wish to browse in a row of cans, film librarians don't need to provide physical access to subjects. Otherwise, they would have to abandon fixed location.

The majority of libraries in the United States have an OPEN SHELF arrangement in which users browse. Most library materials are packaged to attract attention and many patrons, once they have found the correct subject area, prefer to select materials personally. In an open shelf library users find call numbers in the catalog that guide them to shelf locations. Call numbers indicate subjects, and materials with related subjects and adjacent call numbers are shelved together. This can only be achieved by a RELATIVE LOCATION system in which items are not fixed to any one position in the library, but can be moved to and fro as required so that new items can be intershelved with others dealing with the same subject. The design of a relative location system remained an unsolved problem for centuries.

CLASSIFICATION

Classification is the putting together of like things, and to catalogers this means the grouping of library materials into subject areas. First, however, there must be agreement on the subjects themselves. Because material in a library can, in theory, represent all the world's store of information, most classification schemes have started with a philosophical division of human knowledge. The most influential scheme was that of Francis Bacon, who in the 17th century divided knowledge into three general categories: history, poetry, and philosophy. Thomas Jefferson, who owned 7,000 volumes, cataloged them according to Bacon's divisions. The Library of Congress acquired this collection in 1815 and retained the classification system until the end of the 19th century.

In 1873 Melvil Dewey was an undergraduate working in the library of Amherst College, which was arranged at that time in a cumbersome fixed location. Dewey was interested in developing a system that would allow for relative location. At that time there was no model he could imitate, for no large library was completely classified. A number of librarians had experimented with schemes based on Bacon's outline, but no one had devised a simple expandable system. Then, "One Sunday during a long sermon by Pres. Stearns, while I lookt stedfastly at him without hearing a word, my mind absorbed in the vital problem, the solution flasht over me so that I jumpt in my seat and came near shouting *Eureka.*" The solution that came to Dewey was the idea of using numbers with decimal points as subject notations. Thus Dewey created a relative location system with a universal notation that is easy to

Dewey Decimal Classification

understand and can be expanded almost indefinitely by adding numbers after the decimal.

During its evolution through 20 editions, and its growth from 48 pages to three volumes, Dewey's classification system has gathered critics. His subject divisions have been found archaic, his thinking ethnocentric, and his outline of knowledge unoriginal. These complaints are beside the point, however, because the system is practical, provides for relative location, furnishes a call number for shelf location, and brings together like works. More libraries use Dewey than any other classification system and it is unlikely that this will change.

Dewey closely supervised each edition and stipulated that a foundation would continue to do so after his death. Today Forest Press, a subsidiary of the Online Computer Library Center (OCLC), works closely with the Library of Congress, and LC cards indicate a DDC notation. The system is now revised periodically.

Library of Congress

Meanwhile, the scheme devised by Thomas Jefferson was in use at the Library of Congress, but when, in 1897, the one and a half million volumes were moved to new quarters, the Library began to assess the merits of the Dewey system, and that of Charles Cutter, whose system can be expanded by using a combination of both letters and numbers. Dewey refused to allow LC to modify his system in any way. Cutter agreed to modification, but died shortly after. LC ultimately used a system of letters and numbers derived from Cutter. Like the DDC, LCC is based on a classification by discipline, but in this case, not so much the entire world of knowledge, but the world of knowledge as represented by the collection in the Library of Congress. As the collection has grown, LCC has expanded, but revisions depend on the needs of the library, not on the expansion of knowledge in general.

LCC is composed of letters and numbers, and uses 26 letters of the alphabet for its main classes. Unlike DDC, which has one schedule and is the invention of one man, LCC has a group of schedules, each produced by a different team. LCC achieves its relative location by using the letters of the alphabet, and allows for 26 main classes. Each class can be subdivided by use of a second alphabet AA–AZ. Each subclass can then be divided arithmetically, 1–9999. More letters and numbers can be added as required.

TK Class number for technology	RG Medicine
9153 A subdivision number	525 Subdivision
G76 "Author number"	F37 "Author number"

Library of Congress cards are printed with LCC numbers, which are used in many academic libraries. Because revisions are continuous, there are a number of schedules—new, revised, and reprinted with changes.

UNIVERSAL DECIMAL CLASSIFICATION (UDC) is not an original scheme, but a derivative of DDC. The UDC, developed in Europe at the end of the 19th century, is a practical classification based, not on theory, but on the problems of retrieving information from pamphlets, reports, and periodicals. It is basically a system for coding information numerically so that an item, once coded and filed, can be readily found from any access point.

The basic notation of UDC is single Arabic numbers, rather than the minimum three of DDC. Thus religions are 2 rather than 200. A period is placed after every three digits. UDC also has auxiliary symbols that indicate some facet of information: time, space, language, documents with two subjects, points of view, relationships, and so on. UDC is an international code and can be used to specify almost any subject.

UDC has been a great success in special libraries and information centers. In libraries, where indexing is the major consideration rather than shelf arrangement, UDC has proved useful. Journals, indexes, and abstracting services, especially in the field of engineering, have also adopted it. It is now obligatory in Russian scientific and technical libraries. It can be used alone, or with other systems, and computer applications are being studied. UDC has both the faults and the strengths of the system from which it derived.

Reader Interest Classification (RIC) was developed by the Detroit Public Library to serve those collections whose users prefer to select materials by browsing. Materials are placed in large groups centered around topics such as "current affairs," "your family," and "the consumer." These groups can be managed in several ways. One alternative is to use the group term in place of the call number on the book and in the catalog cards. This means the arrangement will be permanent. Another way is to pencil in temporary markings that can be erased when the material is returned to the general collection.

RIC has been used in bookmobiles, small branch libraries, and collections for children and young adults. Little information has been collected on its usefulness, but many librarians have reported positive results. However, almost all libraries cater to topical interests by means of exhibits or temporary groupings, and this seems more practical than committing a collection to permanent RIC classification.

Other classification schemes exist, most of them the work of individuals who attempted to create a perfect system. Even if a perfect classification scheme were devised, however, it is doubtful whether any library would adopt it. Because DDC and LCC

Universal Decimal Classification

Reader Interest Classification

numbers are so readily available in the form of MARC, CIP, and purchased cards, libraries are able to save time that would otherwise be spent on classification. Furthermore, few libraries are willing to spend money on reclassification. During the 1960s, a number of libraries changed from DDC to LCC but that trend has slowed. Indeed, many librarians question the cost of any reclassification, even when this is done to adapt to a new revision of a schedule.

SUBJECT HEADINGS

Classification schemes make it possible to shelve similar subjects together, but this does not solve all problems of subject access. Users must be able to find which notations have been assigned to a given subject; they must have access to materials that cover more than one topic; and they should be aware of what a library has on a given subject.

The problems of subject catalogs have also been studied for many years. Headings derived from titles and from catchwords, and broad headings with subdivisions, have been tried. The theory of SPECIFIC SUBJECT ENTRY was not defined until Cutter had described the two principal objectives of the catalog—to identify works individually and as part of a group. Subject heading theory requires that a work be assigned as specific a subject heading as can be identified. So that the user will be aware of all other material the library has on the subject, headings are not made up by the librarian, but chosen from a standard list.

Subject control is easier to achieve in theory than in reality, because neither the cataloger nor the user can be sure how the other is going to interpret a subject, or what words may have been chosen for access. Catalogers can reduce confusion by using standard lists and by creating a network of *see* and *see also* references. Still, choosing a subject heading is often challenging.

Types of Subject Headings

The simplest subject heading is a noun. The user searching for information on tigers will probably look for the heading "tigers." This type of subject heading usually causes few problems, but the singular and the plural of a noun may have different meanings, for example, drama and dramas, theater and theaters. Bridge can be a game or a structure. There is also the problem of those who will look for tigers under "animals" or even "mammals."

Some noun headings are expanded with adjectives in order to make them more specific. This creates another problem: will users look under the adjective or the noun? Because opinions have differed, both "American literature" and "Philosophy, Chinese" can be found.

Some subjects are so closely related that compound headings are necessary, for example, "technology and civilization," "cities and towns," "clocks and watches." Even if this concept is correct, there remains the problem of which word comes first.

Other concepts require a phrase in order to be specific: "acting for television," "social problems in literature," "drama in education." Subject headings can also be made more specific by adding place, literary form, or period, a process referred to as subdivision.

Automation makes possible another subject retrieval approach. Through KEYWORD SEARCHES individual words in any selected field of the bibliographic citation can serve as access points. For example, "conservation of natural resources" is a standard subject heading and if typed (without error) into an interactive catalog retrieves items so indexed. However, conservation and resources, or even the truncated terms conserv? and resour? also retrieve information in many databases. This broader approach not only searches subject headings, but also other fields such as titles and notes. Subject headings still provide the most specific information, however, especially in large databases. And while computers can aid the process, especially in generating cross references, human catalogers will be responsible for providing subject access for most library materials in the foreseeable future.

PRECIS (Preserved Context Index System) is a computer-assisted system developed by the British National Bibliography during the 1960s and used to index a variety of bibliographies and catalogs for both print and nonprint formats, especially in British Commonwealth countries. In PRECIS, a subject heading is replaced by a "string," a series of terms summarizing the content of a work. Each term in the string is related to the terms immediately preceding and following it. Terms are recorded starting with the widest context and moving to the most specific. For example, a string for a work dealing with evaluation of management in industry in Japan presents the subject in summary form as follows:

PRECIS

Japan—industry—management—evaluation

Any or every term in the string can serve as the entry term for the user. The terms are kept in logical order so the links between them are not broken. A two-line entry structure is employed.

| LEAD | Qualifier |

| Display |

The lead is the term that functions as the entry point for the user. The qualifiers place the lead in successively wider contexts. The display is a term of narrower reference.

MANAGEMENT. — Industry. — Japan.
Evaluation.

INDUSTRY. — Japan.
Management. Evaluation.

The indexers put only a single string into the computer, which contains instructions on how the terms should be manipulated into entries; the address to which the entries refer; and all the *see* and *see also* references (called RINS, or Reference Indicator Numbers) appropriate to the terms in the string.

Once the record has entered the computer, the human task is completed and the machine takes over. Not only does it generate all indicated entries and references, but it also sorts and generates a magnetic tape which can be used to create catalogs and other bibliographic products.

SUBJECT HEADING LISTS

Catalogers assign subject headings by using a standard subject heading list, hoping that, by following its directives, they will be able to guide most library users successfully.

The most commonly used subject heading lists are *Library of Congress Subject Headings* (LCSH) and the *Sears List of Subject Headings*. LCSH, first published in 1909 and now in its 13th edition, is a list of subject headings used in the Library of Congress. These subject headings are also printed on LC cards, on MARC tapes, and in the Cataloging in Publication data found on the verso of the title page of a book. General directions for using the list are printed in the introduction. *Sears*, first published in 1923, is intended for small general collections.

Special libraries, which deal with particular subject areas in depth, need more specific terms than those provided by either of these general lists. Medical libraries, for example, use MeSH (Medical Subject Headings) and other fields have similar lists. MeSH was developed by the National Library of Medicine as part of its computer retrieval system and is not so much a subject heading list as a THESAURUS. As more and more subject searches are being done with the aid of the computer, other databases have developed thesauri for strictly limited subject areas such as the ERIC (Educational Resources Information Center) thesaurus. Even when no computer is involved, many groups publish specialized lists to be used in conjunction with a general list, and religious denominations often publish and update such lists regularly in their journals.

Special lists are developed for special interests, but general lists attempt to provide subject access for library users in general, and must therefore sacrifice precision and topicality. LCSH and Sears are revised periodically, but revision is an expensive and time-consuming chore not to be undertaken lightly. Long after travelers were flying in jets, LCSH was guiding them to information under the heading "aeroplane."

When, during the late 1960s, minority groups and women began to assert that social prejudice is reflected in language, subject heading lists were accused of bias. Librarians have long been aware that the Dewey classification scheme is biased and revisions have been made to overcome this problem. Yet it is difficult to imagine a user becoming incensed over a call number no matter what bias it might express to the librarian. Such headings in the public catalog as "NEGROES—SOCIAL AND MORAL CONDITION," "DELINQUENT WOMEN," and "JEWS AS DOCTORS" are a different matter. These and other headings have now been revised. Users are entitled to subject headings that are not only useful but also appear impartial, and catalogers should attempt to make subject headings reflect current social conditions.

SUMMARY

Department stores, supermarkets, and libraries all try to classify their contents so the patrons can find and compare the items they want. While department stores must categorize the apparel they sell, libraries have a more difficult task. A library contains a large part of the accumulated wisdom of the world, and the information needs of users are not as easily measured as their clothing sizes. By using a notation system, classification provides call numbers that locate each item according to subject. The two most popular systems in the United States are the Dewey Decimal, which uses numbers and decimals, and the Library of Congress, which combines letters and numbers. The user can locate these call numbers by searching for subject headings or descriptors in a catalog. To provide for standardization these headings are selected from printed lists such as *Sears* or the *Library of Congress Subject Headings* list. Specialized lists also exist to give access to collections that need more detailed analysis.

CHAPTER REVIEW

Terms to understand:

closed shelf	PRECIS
fixed location	relative location
keyword search	specific subject entry
open shelf	thesaurus

Classification schemes:

Provide notations so that subjects can be shelved together.

DDC — Dewey Decimal Classification
LCC — Library of Congress Classification
UDC — Universal Decimal Classification
RIC — Reader Interest Classification

Subject headings:

Locate items individually with a specific subject entry.

Are standardized so that subjects can be gathered together in the catalog.

May be single nouns, nouns with adjectives, compound headings, or phrases, and can be subdivided for greater accuracy.

General libraries select from a general list (LCSH or *Sears*). Special libraries use specialized lists. Computer retrieval systems use thesauri.

PRECIS replaces subject headings with a string of relevant and connected terms. The computer selects *see* and *see also* references for these terms and produces the completed records.

CHAPTER 8

CLASSIFYING WITH DEWEY

THE DEWEY Decimal Classification (DDC) is almost synonymous with librarianship in the minds of the public. School children learn the ten classification areas and the general reader is comfortable with them. The Dewey tables are easy to work with, the scheme can be expanded to suit a collection of any size, and cataloging copy with Dewey numbers is available in many printed sources. No wonder the DDC is used all over the world and has been translated into many languages, including Chinese.

GENERAL GUIDELINES FOR CLASSIFICATION

The purpose of classification is to arrange a collection, not place a single item. Users who browse expect to find like subjects together. An efficient arrangement depends on familiarity with a collection, its contents, the reasons for its existence, and the purpose of its users.

In classification the first step is to identify the subject for the item in hand. During the technical reading the title is identified. Because it is risky to depend on the title alone in subject analysis, the table of contents and all available introductory material are examined, but catalogers rarely need to examine the entire contents of an item in order to determine a subject.

Determine where items with similar subjects have been placed in the collection by checking the catalog. The cataloger may have a choice of classification numbers, but, remembering the user, should be consistent in assigning notations.

As noted in Chapter 7, most items can be assigned more than one subject heading. When an item deals with several subjects, classify under the dominant one or, when this cannot be determined, under the first mentioned in the text. When there are more than three subjects, classify under the more general topic. For example, a book of essays discussing mathematics, physics, chemistry, and biology should be classified in general science. The DDC usually gives instructions for such comprehensive works.

Never be tempted to make up a number for a subject that is not included in the tables, because future editions may use that number for another topic. Simply use the most specific notation in the tables that covers the subject. The DDC schedules are frequently revised to reflect changes in the nature of subjects and disciplines, but cannot be completely up-to-date with current events and discoveries. New subjects are usually included in the schedules by re-assigning or expanding notations. When this happens the cataloger can decide to leave the topic in the general number, or, if a great deal of material has accumulated, to be more specific by reclassifying to the new number.

In general, the cataloger is advised to place a work where it is most useful. While the beginning cataloger may have little idea where this might be, experience with the schedules and knowledge of the collection and its users improves classification skills.

DEWEY DECIMAL CLASSIFICATION

The DDC is published in both abridged and unabridged editions. The abridged DDC shortens the numbers of the larger edition and is intended for small general collections of 20,000 items or fewer. Both editions include SCHEDULES, TABLES, and a RELATIVE INDEX. Any library, however, may house special collections that need precise subject division. In that case the notations of the unabridged edition can be used in those areas only.

Although the following discussion refers primarily to the 11th abridged edition, some examples of special uses for the 20th edition are illustrated.

DDC divides all knowledge into ten main classes (Figure 8-1). The first of the three digits indicates the class:

000	Generalities	500	Pure sciences
100	Philosophy and related disciplines	600	Technology (Applied sciences)
		700	The arts
200	Religion	800	Literature (Belles-lettres)
300	Social sciences	900	General geography and
400	Language		history

Figure 8-1

Each main class comprises ten divisions (Figure 8-2). The second digit indicates the division:

700 The arts
- 710 Civic & landscape art
- 720 Architecture
- 730 Plastic arts Sculpture
- 740 Drawing, decorative & minor arts
- 750 Painting and paintings
- 760 Graphic arts Prints
- 770 Photography & photographs
- 780 Music
- 790 Recreational & performing arts

Figure 8-2

Each division has ten sections (Figure 8-3). The third digit indicates the section:

700 The arts
701 Philosophy & theory
702 Miscellany
703 Dictionaries & encyclopedias
704 Special topics of general applicability
705 Serial publications
706 Organizations & management
707 Study & teaching
708 Galleries, museums, art collections
709 Historical & geographical treatment

Figure 8-3

Topics are covered more specifically by subsequent divisions of the section (Figure 8-4):

750 Painting & paintings
751 Processes & forms
752 Color
753 Abstractions, symbolism, legend
754 Subjects of everyday life
755 Religion & religious symbolism
756 Historical events
757 Human figures & their parts
758 Other subjects
759 Historical & geographical treatment

760 Graphic arts   Prints
761 Relief processes
762
763 Lithographic processes
764 Serigraphy & chromolithography
765 Metal engraving
766 Mezzotinting & aquatinting processes
767 Etching & drypoint
768
769 Prints

Figure 8-4

The blank spaces indicate that numbers included in earlier editions have been dropped from the schedule. In future editions, these numbers will be assigned to other subjects. Classification relationships change to reflect changes in knowledge itself. Each edition warns when numbers have been dropped and subjects in that section moved elsewhere in the table. The assumption is that if numbers are left vacant long enough, the existing materials will wear out, or become outdated, and when the number is used again, little material will require reclassification. Dewey once promised that numbers would be left vacant for 25 years, but that has proved impossible.

The decimal point allows numbers within a class to expand as they are further subdivided. Notice how this works in "processes and forms of painting" (Figure 8-5):

751   Processes and forms

Class processes and forms of individual painters in 759.1–759.9

▶   **751.2–751.6 Techniques, procedures, apparatus, equipment, materials**

Class comprehensive works in 750.28

.2   **Materials**

Surfaces, pigments, mediums, fixatives, coatings

Class use of materials in specific techniques in 751.4

.3   **Apparatus, equipment, artists' models**

Class use of apparatus and equipment in specific techniques in 751.4

.4   **Techniques and procedures**

Painting with specific mediums

Including collage (with painting as the basic technique), airbrush painting

Class mosaic painting [*formerly* 751.4] in 738.5

For techniques of reproduction, see 751.5

.42   **Watercolor painting**

Do not use standard subdivisions

.45   **Oil painting**

.5   **Techniques of reproduction**

Execution, identification, determination of authenticity of reproductions, copies, forgeries, alterations

For printmaking and prints, see 760

.6   **Conservation, preservation, restoration, routine care**

Including expertizing

Class identification of reproductions, copies, forgeries, alterations in 751.5

.7   **Specific forms**

Examples: easel paintings, murals, panoramas, theatrical scenery, miniatures

Class specific subjects in specific forms in 753–758; techniques, procedures, apparatus, equipment, materials employed in specific forms in 751.2–751.6

Figure 8-5

Further subdivision of 751 from the 20th unabridged edition (Figure 8-6):

751   **Techniques, procedures, apparatus, equipment, materials [*formerly* 750.28], forms**

.2   **Materials**

Examples: surfaces, pigments, mediums, fixatives, coatings

Class use of materials in specific techniques in 751.4

.3   **Apparatus, equipment, artists' models**

Class use of apparatus and equipment in specific techniques in 751.4

.4   **Techniques and procedures**

.42   Use of water-soluble mediums

For tempera painting, see 751.43

.422   Watercolor painting

Including casein painting, gouache

Class ink painting in color in 751.425

.422 4   Watercolor painting techniques by subject

Add to base number 751.4224 the numbers following 704.94 in 704.942–704.949, e.g., techniques of landscape painting in watercolor 751.422436

.425   Ink painting

.425 1   Chinese ink painting

.425 14   Chinese ink painting techniques by subject

Add to base number 751.42514 the numbers following 704.94 in 704.942–704.949, e.g., techniques of landscape painting in Chinese ink painting 751.4251436

.425 2   Japanese ink painting

.426   Acrylic painting

.43   Tempera painting

.44   Fresco painting

.45   Oil painting

.454   Oil painting techniques by subject

Add to base number 751.454 the numbers following 704.94 in 704.942–704.949, e.g., techniques of landscape painting in oils 751.45436

.46   Encaustic (Wax) painting

.49   Other methods

Examples: finger, polymer, roller (brayer), sand painting

Class mosaic painting in 738.5

.493   Collage

Figure 8-6

When a library has only a few items in a class, and does not plan to acquire more, it is possible to use a more general number. A special library, for example, may own only five or six books in the discipline "The Arts" and could choose to classify them all under 700. A small general collection would probably have enough materials on painting and paintings to use the number 750, which has only three subdivisions, but not the number 751. A larger collection might need to classify more precisely, using 751 for processes and forms, 755 for religious symbolism, and so forth. If the size of the collection warrants, 751—"Processes and forms"—can be further divided by using decimals. Note that techniques of watercolor and oil painting each have their own numbers, but could be classified together under 751.4. In a large collection, users will be able to find materials more easily if the minute distinctions of the unabridged edition, which even supplies a number for finger-painting, are followed. Contrast 751.4—"Techniques and procedures"—in the abridged edition with 751.4—"Techniques and procedures"—in the unabridged edition, in which many more specific topics have notations created by expanding numbers.

An art library can decide to use the unabridged edition for the art materials only, but classify other subjects in the collection with the abridged edition. Special collections, in which knowledgeable users seek special information, should probably be cataloged with the unabridged edition. A collection focusing on state or local history, regardless of its size, uses the unabridged edition because it provides a specific number for each county. Classifiers arrange materials for profitable browsing. As collections grow it is easier for users to browse when more specific numbers are used. Keep in mind shelf arrangement when classifying.

Dewey tables also provide SCOPE NOTES, directions, and examples (Figure 8-7). No matter which edition of Dewey is used it is extremely important to read such material and follow the instructions.

.5   Macroeconomic policy

Economic stabilization and growth, incomes policies, full employment policies; use of fiscal policy, e.g., government spending, budget surpluses and deficits, taxation; use of monetary policy, e.g., discount rates offered by central banks, reserve requirements imposed on banks, open market operations, regulation of bank credit

Including income redistribution, transfer payments

Class measures to combat inflation in 332.4, to control economic fluctuations in 338.5, to promote growth and development in 338.9

Figure 8-7

The Relative Index

After the subject of the item in hand has been identified, the class number is located. Often prepared copy and purchased cards provide numbers, and the *Sears* subject list has abridged numbers. Check the RELATIVE INDEX and the library's shelf list before using numbers from prepared copy. This assures the number fits the existing shelf arrangement for numbers printed on copy. The index of the DDC is called a relative index because it gives not only numbers, but also the relationships between topics.

An example from the relative index shows how aspects of a single subject, economics, may be dispersed throughout the schedules (Figure 8-8). The history of economics is 330.9, but the economic aspects of geology are found under 553, a science notation. After

Economic	
assistance internat.	
see Foreign aid	
biology	574.6
animals	591.6
plants	581.6
botany	581.6
conditions	330.9
fluctuations	338.5
geography	330.91–.99
geology	553
growth	
macroeconomics	339.5
history	330.9
institutions	
sociology	306
order	
soc. theology	
Christianity	261.8
comp. rel.	291.1
planning	338.9
rent land econ.	333.01
resources *see* Resources	
rights	
pol. sci.	323.4
situation	330.9
stabilization	
macroeconomics	339.5
zoology	591.6

Figure 8-8

selecting a possible notation from the index, check the number in the tables. If 339.5 has been tentatively selected for a book on government economic policy, turn to that number, where a scope note explains which topics may be placed there.

Note that measures to combat inflation are not classed in this number but in 332.4. Never attempt to classify from the index alone; always check the tables and read all scope notes.

Classification is generally by subject, but within subjects certain sub-arrangements are possible. These sub-arrangements are presented in AUXILIARY TABLES (Figure 8-9). There are four such tables in the abridged edition:

Auxiliary Tables

Table 1: standard subdivisions
Table 2: areas
Table 3: subdivisions of individual literatures
Table 4: subdivisions of individual languages

Figure 8-9

Table 3 is used only with the 800s (literature) and table 4 with the 400s (language).

The notations in Table 1 (Figure 8-10), STANDARD SUBDIVISIONS, may be added to any DDC number unless directions explicitly state: "Do not use standard subdivisions."

SUMMARY

—01   **Philosophy and theory**
—02   **Miscellany**
—03   **Dictionaries, encyclopedias, concordances**
—04   **Special topics of general applicability**
—05   **Serial publications**
—06   **Organizations and management**
—07   **Study and teaching**
—09   **Historical and geographical treatment**

Figure 8-10

Suppose that a book on government economic policy is a book of definitions of terms. The notation tentatively chosen for that topic is 339.5. To group dictionaries together within the topic the number can be expanded with the standard subdivision number 03, forming the notation 339.503.

If the work is a history of macroeconomic policy the notation is 339.509. Standard subdivisions are indicated with a zero. Unless directed, do not use more than one, no matter where the decimal point falls. For example, the correct notation for how to teach science is 507 *not* 500.7 or 500.07. How to teach science of the earth is 550.7 *not* 550.07.

One of the most commonly used standard subdivisions is 09, which denotes historical and geographical treatment of a subject. To indicate a biography, the number should be lengthened to 092.

Biographies can be classified in a separate section, or placed with related subject matter. The second practice is followed at the Library of Congress and many academic libraries, where a biography of Queen Victoria would be found in English history, a biography of Hank Aaron in the baseball section, and a biography of a surgeon in the medical area. Public libraries have customarily marked biographies with a B and shelved them in a general biography section. This would probably not be a good policy in a collection that serves many kinds of research needs. A student writing on the unification of Germany would expect to find biographies of Bismarck with German history, and a reader with an interest in the French Revolution will look for biographies of the famous participants among other works on the subject. Similarly, high school students who want to read about tennis stars will be better served when these books are shelved with other tennis books, rather than scattered through the general biography section. A biography should not be routinely assigned to one general section, however. For example, 792 is the notation for Theater (stage presentations). Biographies of famous theater personalities arranged under 792.092 are easily found. This method of arrangement does not preclude maintaining a general biography section containing biographies for recreational reading.

Sometimes the coverage of a topic may be limited to a single geographical area. If the collection contains a great deal of material on a particular subject, the cataloger may decide to subdivide the subject by place using the AREA TABLES (Figure 8-11).

Area Tables

Table 2. Areas

SUMMARY

—1 Areas, regions, places in general
—2 Persons regardless of area, region, place
—3 The ancient world
—4 Europe   Western Europe
—5 Asia   Orient   Far East
—6 Africa
—7 North America
—8 South America
—9 Other parts of world and extraterrestrial worlds   Pacific Ocean islands (Oceania)

Figure 8-11

The schedules often give the instruction "add area notations." When there are no such instructions, area notations may still be added by placing 09 from Table 1 in front of the area number (Figure 8-12). Suppose the collection contains many items concerning the macroeconomic policies of governments. These can be arranged by regions. Because there are no directions at 339.5 about using area codes, 09 will be used with the proper notations.

macroeconomic policy in Japan   339.5 macroeconomic policy
      339.50952   09   standard subdivision
                                      52   area number for Japan

Figure 8-12

When instructions read "add area" notation, as they do at 549.9 (geographical distribution of minerals), the area number is added directly to the class number 549.9. For example, geographical distribution of minerals in Japan is 549.952.

Table 3 and
Table 4

    Table 3 applies only to the literature schedule and is used with numbers 810–890. This table divides literature collections according to their form. Table 4, for the language schedule, is used with numbers 420–490 and, within particular languages, distinguishes between dictionaries, grammars, and readers.

Language and
Literature
(including fiction)
Tables

    Although the disciplines of language and literature are closely related, these two areas are widely separated on the shelves in the DDC system. The 400s and the 800s are structured in much the same way, however, and both contain MNEMONIC DEVICES to assist classification and shelf location (Figure 8-13). Note that the second digit in the number denotes the same language in either class, and that, in the subdivisions, the third digit denotes the literary form.

Summary of the Two General Classes

400 Language		800 Literature (Belles-lettres)	
410	Linguistics	810	American literature in English
420	English & Anglo-Saxon languages	820	English & Anglo-Saxon literatures
430	Germanic languages German	830	Literatures of Germanic languages
440	Romance languages French	840	Literatures of Romance languages
450	Italian, Romanian, Rhaeto-Romanic	850	Italian, Romanian, Rhaeto-Romanic
460	Spanish & Portuguese languages	860	Spanish & Portuguese literatures
470	Italic languages Latin	870	Italic literatures Latin
480	Hellenic Classical Greek	880	Hellenic literatures Greek
490	Other languages	890	Literatures of other languages

Subdivisions

420 English & Anglo-Saxon languages		430 Germanic languages German	
421	Written & spoken English	431	Written & spoken German
422	English etymology	432	German etymology
423	English dictionaries	433	German dictionaries
424		434	
425	English structural system	435	German structural system
426		436	
427	Nonstandard English	437	Nonstandard German
428	Standard English usage	438	Standard German usage
429	Anglo-Saxon (Old English)	439	Other Germanic languages

820 English & Anglo-Saxon literatures		830 Literatures of Germanic languages	
821	English poetry	831	German poetry
822	English drama	832	German drama
823	English fiction	833	German fiction
824	English essays	834	German essays
825	English speeches	835	German speeches
826	English letters	836	German letters
827	English satire & humor	837	German satire & humor
828	English miscellaneous writings	838	German miscellaneous writings
829	Anglo-Saxon (Old English)	839	Other Germanic literatures

           Figure 8-13

The first number indicates discipline:

    4 = Language   8 = Literature

The second number indicates nationality:

    42 = Language   English & Anglo-Saxon

    82 = Literature   English & Anglo-Saxon

The third number indicates form:

    423 = Language   English dictionaries

    823 = Literature   English fiction

To use the tables in either section, first locate the BASE NUMBER in the schedules.

The base number is made up of the number indicating discipline and the number indicating language, and is identified from the schedules. Once the base number is located turn to the proper table—e.g., Table 4 for the 400s and Table 3 for the eight hundreds—to find the correct notation for form.

To classify a book of humorous stories in German:

Literature

Base number for German = 83

Table 3 — satire and humor collections of more than one author = 7008

Added to the base number = 837.008

Language

A graded German reader would be classified in the 400s from the schedule:

Base number — German language = 43

From the tables:

    Readers (graded selection) = 86

    A graded German reader = 438.6

In most libraries the 400 section, even including the dictionaries, is a small section. Classification can probably be done from the general schedules without expanding the tables. The literature section, the 800s, is much larger, more complicated to arrange, and requires more attention.

The 800s reflect certain of Dewey's assumptions, as do other sections. He assumed that the major literatures of the world had been identified and could be conveniently arranged between 810 and 880, leaving 890 for other national literatures that might appear. This has led to the present situation in the abridged DDC, in which the literature of more than 70 languages is crowded between 890 and 899. In this span the system of base numbers breaks down, and only a base number for Russian is identified—891.7. A large literature collection is better arranged using the unabridged edition.

Literature Shelf
Arrangement

Dewey also envisioned fiction shelved in the 800s, according to language of composition, and provided the form digit 3 for this. Most libraries, however, prefer to classify fiction separately with F or Fic used in place of a DDC number. This normally works quite well. Some fictional works, however, are better classed in the DDC numbers. An example is fiction written in a language other than English. The patron looking for a novel in German or Italian should not have to search the entire fiction section, but only among novels in those languages. It is more convenient to place novels written in French in 843 than somewhere in F. High school and college libraries can also consider placing study texts of novels in the 800 classification, because these are not suitable for casual reading, but are intended for the literature student. This number can also be considered for biographies of novelists, adding, of course, 092. A biography of Hemingway would therefore be shelved 813.092. A critical analysis of Hemingway's novels would also be shelved in 813. A library could choose to put popular editions of Hemingway's novels in the F section, but critical analysis and study editions of the works in 813 beside those books concerned with his life. This arrangement places works logically for users. Although separated on the shelves, Hemingway materials are still related in the catalog under the access point for Hemingway.

Although Shakespeare has his own notation (822.3), shelving the vast amount of material concerning this author is a problem even in small collections. The unabridged DDC has a table for arranging the works of Shakespeare which can be adapted for use with any author and could be used with the abridged edition as a guide for shelving Shakespeare and other writers (Figure 8-14).

A	Authorship controversies
	(It is optional to class here bibliography; prefer 016.82233)
B	Biography
D	Critical appraisal
	Class critical appraisal of individual works in O-Z
E	Textual criticism
	Class textual criticism of individual works in O-Z
F	Sources, allusions, learning
G	Societies, concordances, miscellany
H	Quotations, condensations, adaptations
I	Complete works in English without notes
J	Complete works in English with notes
K	Complete works in translation
L	Partial collections in English without notes
M	Partial collections in English with notes
N	Partial collections in translation
▶O-Z	Individual works

Figure 8-14

A work dealing with authorship controversies would be 822.3A; a biography of Shakespeare, 822.3B. Literary criticism of the poet T. S. Eliot would be 821E; his poetry would be shelved in 821I or 821J.

Even when all fiction is separated in "Fic" it is often necessary to subdivide it further. Many readers enjoy short stories, but would not want to browse the whole fiction section to find them. Short stories can be shelved separately, marked SC for Story Collection, or given a DDC number and shelved with other literary forms. Fiction is more often selected by browsing than nonfiction. Some patrons want only mysteries, others only romance. Special fiction collections in such popular subjects can be maintained for those readers.

The 900 section (Figure 8-15) is not as complex as the 800s, but it is also a large area, and concepts used in the 800s to save space in the schedules are also employed here. Again, the first step is identifying the subject, whether history as a discipline (900–909) or geography as a discipline (910–912) or general geography (913–919) or general history (930–999).

General History and Geography

900	**General geography & history**	**940**	**General history of Europe**
910	General geography Travel	941	British Isles
920	General biography & genealogy	942	England & Wales
930	General history of ancient world	943	Central Europe Germany
940	General history of Europe	944	France & Monaco
950	General history of Asia	945	Italy
960	General history of Africa	946	Iberian Peninsula Spain
970	General history of North America	947	Soviet Union
980	General history of South America	948	Scandinavia
990	General history of other areas	949	Other parts of Europe

910 General geography   Travel

911	Historical geography
912	Graphic representations of earth
913	Geography of ancient world
914	Europe
915	Asia
916	Africa
917	North America
918	South America
919	Other areas & worlds

Figure 8-15

Any work that deals with geography and travel in the ancient and modern world can be classified using the base number 91 and the correct notation from Table 2, the area notation table (Figure 8-16). If the approach is historical, rather than geographical, the base number is 9 plus the correct notation from area 2. A travel book entitled *What's Doing in England* is assigned 914.2, whereas a history of England is 942.

Summary—from Table 2. Areas.

—41 British Isles
—42 England and Wales
—43 Central Europe   Germany
—44 France and Monaco
—45 Italy
—46 Iberian Peninsula and adjacent islands   Spain
—47 Union of Soviet Socialist Republics (Soviet Union)
—48 Scandinavia
—49 Other parts of Europe

Figure 8-16

The history section will usually be much larger than the geography section and must be subdivided by historical periods if users are to browse with ease. United States history (973) is subdivided by chronological periods, and after the 20th century, by terms of individual presidents; e.g., 973.924 is President Nixon, 973.925 is Ford, and 973.926 is Carter. The current edition lists no notation for President Reagan's administration but the correct one can easily be added. Since this span to 973.999 may be used for individual presidents, catalogers need not worry about running out of notations until the 22nd century.

There is a close connection between history and biography, for a biography is a history of an individual. The 900 schedule provides a span for classification of biography, both general and specific. In reality, few libraries use this span [920–928], preferring either to mark the materials "B," or classify with a specific discipline using the standard subdivision notation 092.

Each library decides how to arrange its collection to make it accessible to patrons. Decisions on where to shelve biographies, how to arrange fiction, and how closely to classify vary from institution to institution, and the DDC schedules themselves do not address these problems. Once a library has established policies the cataloger should have little difficulty in applying any section of the DDC correctly, provided that all scope notes and directions are carefully followed.

Selecting a DDC classification notation does not complete the call number. A number of items may share a classification number, depending on which subjects are in the collection. In general, a BOOK NUMBER is used to achieve alphabetical arrangement within the classification. Most libraries try to assign a unique call number to each item. The call number is made up of a classification number and a book number whose notation is based on the main entry. Materials are shelved alphabetically according to main entry (excluding articles if a title) or, in the case of biographies, the subject's last name, thus assuring that works about people will be found together. Call numbers are recorded in the catalog and are marked on the item where they can be seen by the patron, for example, on the spine of a book. Many libraries simply add the first three letters of the main entry, or subject, or author's name underneath the classification to create the call number. Large collections may use a Cutter "author table" to provide a letter-number combination book number. These tables were first developed by Charles Cutter and later revised by Kate Sanborn to supply book numbers for the DDC. These tables are alphabetical arrangements by name or a shortened form of the name, each with a number behind it. For example, the name Groff will be found in a long list of Gs with the number 893 beside it (Figure 8-17). The Cutter number for Groff will be G893 and would be added beneath a DDC number to form a call number.

Book Numbers	
Gro	89
Grobe	891
Groco	892
Groff	893
Groh	894
Groll	895
Grolm	896
Gromi	897
Grone	898
Groom	899
Gyo	998

Figure 8-17

DDC number 973 call number	973 call number
G893 Cutter table	GRO using first 3
	letters of
	main entry

A CUTTER TABLE is simple to use and keeps a collection in excellent order. It will take longer to look up names in the table, however, than it will to use the first three letters only. Cutter never envisioned that many works would be entered by title, but today title main entry is common. It is difficult, but not impossible, to use the table with other than proper names. Although use of the Cutter tables may take longer initially, it can save shelving time.

Each library must decide whether it would be feasible to use staff time to create an alphabetical shelf order. In a small collection a classification number may be enough, especially for nonfiction. Even in a small library, however, fiction is another matter, and these materials are often not kept in good order, even when marked with three letters. Cutter may be used only with fiction, which is normally shelved by author anyway. More markings can be added as desired; for example, an author's novels can be kept in alphabetical order by title by adding lower-case letters to the book number.

> Hemingway—For Whom the Bell Tolls   H375f
>   The Sun Also Rises   H375s

Some libraries mark fiction with the entire last name of the author on the spine to ensure correct shelving. Publication date can be added below for clarification.

In research libraries many users search in the catalog and then on the shelf for a specific work. In large collections, an item marked with only three letters might be difficult to find. In such cases a unique call number is extremely important and time should be taken to provide one. If a collection is very small and will probably remain so, or if material is mainly located by browsing, any system that provides a rough alphabetical order may be sufficient.

Reclassification

One limitation of a classification scheme based on the present state of knowledge is that knowledge changes, grows, and shifts emphasis. Such a scheme will soon cease to reflect what people are studying, reading, watching, or acquiring for libraries. The scheme of knowledge outlined in the first DDC tables (1876) has been thoroughly superseded and in each subsequent edition topics have been relocated, discontinued, expanded, or even created anew in PHOENIX SCHEDULES. Dewey assumed that the major disciplines were established for all time, and so used all the numbers in his schedules without planning for expansion. The problem is evident in each section and can be easily understood by looking at the 100s and 200s (Figure 8-18).

100 Philosophy & related disciplines
110   Metaphysics
120   Epistemology, causation, humankind
130   Paranormal phenomena & arts
140   Specific philosophical viewpoints
150   Psychology
160   Logic
170   Ethics (Moral philosophy)
180   Ancient, medieval, Oriental
190   Modern Western philosophy

200 Religion
210   Natural religion
220   Bible
230   Christian theology
240   Christian moral & devotional
250   Local church & religious orders
260   Social & ecclesiastical theology
270   History & geography of church
280   Christian denominations & sects
290   Other & comparative religions

Figure 8-18

In the 1870s psychology was hardly acknowledged as a field of study and Dewey allowed it only one span of numbers. The rest of the 100s was taken up with philosophy. Contemporary librarians need the imbalance reversed to reflect the contents of their collections. In the 11th abridged edition the 150s take up one third of the entire 100 schedule.

Dewey assumed that by leaving 290 for religions other than

Christianity he had provided as many spans as any library would need. As a result the present abridged edition assigns ten specific religions and all religions of Black Africa and of Native American origin to 299.

Successive editors of the DDC have tried to produce schedules that reflect current needs. At present a new edition is prepared every seven years. Without exception, each edition makes a great many changes, presenting the cataloger with the problem of whether to reclassify every time DDC changes numbers.

Reclassification is not a job to be undertaken lightly because hours must be spent changing the notation in every place that it appears. Some librarians are vociferous in their opposition to reclassification, claiming it is not worth the time or money to shift items on a shelf. This school of thought adopts an edition of Dewey and sticks with it. At the other end of the spectrum are those who feel it necessary to reclassify with each edition in order to keep classification consistent with current knowledge. Most librarians take a middle course, perhaps classifying new arrivals according to the latest edition, but not reclassifying older material. This means users will not be able to browse easily for a while, but eventually much of the material in the older section can be discarded, and the remainder reclassified. Others might ignore minor changes, but reclassify when a major relocation or a Phoenix schedule appears. Reclassification is a decision that is made by weighing available resources against the needs of users.

SUMMARY

When catalogers choose main and added entries, they are influenced by the desire to standardize the identification of items from library to library. However, DDC notations are chosen so that an individual collection can be arranged to support the needs of the users, whether they require research materials or a good mystery. Large, specialized, or research libraries rely on the unabridged DDC for precise classification, whereas small general libraries with less than 20,000 items will find the more general numbers in the abridged edition adequate. Even a small library may need precise classification for specialized collections, and it is appropriate to employ the unabridged edition when preparing these materials.

Locating subject notations in DDC is not difficult, but it is important to read and follow the directions. Consult the index, find a number in the schedule, and check the shelf list to ensure that like subjects will be found together on the shelf. Certain subarrangements can be achieved within the subject area by using the auxiliary tables. Again, it is extremely important to follow the directions when subdividing.

Certain decisions about classification remain for the cataloger. These are made on the basis of the "convenience of the public," which in the case of classification is their browsing convenience. There are, for example, various options when classifying biographies and fiction. Because the literature section houses such diverse materials it can be confusing to arrange, and some logical shelving scheme has to be worked out. Book numbers must be added to the DDC to complete call numbers and to achieve alphabetical order on the shelf. Achieving perfect order requires time; the librarian balances time available against the requirements for order.

No classification system is perfect, and librarians have limited resources and time. Yet bringing order out of the chaotic world of information is one of the most important responsibilities of the profession and classification can be a key to fulfilling it.

CHAPTER REVIEW

Terms to understand:

area tables	Phoenix schedule
auxiliary tables	relative index
base number	schedules
book number	scope note
Cutter table	standard subdivision
mnemonic devices	tables

In classification:

Be consistent.
Follow a schedule.

Dewey Decimal Classification:

The Abridged Edition—for small general collections.
The Unabridged Edition—for large collections or special collections.

Consult the relative index, find the notation in the schedules, carefully read scope notes and directions. Check catalog.

Policies determined by each library:

How to class biographies.
How to arrange the literature section.
Assignment of book numbers.
When to reclassify.

CLASSIFICATION gives an item a shelf address, locating it among other materials within the same general subject. Catalogers then provide fine-tuned content access by assigning subject headings. A title can have only one shelf location, but can be accessed in the catalog via as many subject headings as the cataloger chooses.

The assignment of both subject headings and classification notations depends on the content of the material. During the technical reading, consider the intellectual content with both processes in mind. The main thrust of the work determines shelf location and suggests a subject heading. Additional topics or aspects indicate further access points for catalog retrieval. The subject headings selected should both lead to the appropriate specific titles in the collection and serve as a gathering device for all titles dealing with similar topics. To do this successfully, headings have to be uniformly applied and a standard list consulted. *Sears* and the *Library of Congress Subject Headings* (LCSH) are the authority lists most commonly used for general collections. As no one can predict exactly what topics a user will search on—i.e., cars or automobiles, flying saucers or UFO's, drug habit or drug abuse—these standard lists provide a network of terms and are laced with cross references to those uniform headings preferred for use.

SEARS AND LCSH

Both of these subject heading tools list topics alphabetically with WORD-BY-WORD FILING. In *Sears* the preferred headings appear in bold-face type. Terms not used appear in ordinary type, followed by a cross reference to the approved uniform term.

Organization and Arrangement

As shown in Figure 9-1, *Sears*, the less complex tool, provides fewer and less complicated terms and is preferred for small general libraries. LCSH is more complex (Figure 9-2) because it expands topic areas into many subdivisions and includes numerous proper nouns as topics. Terms are coordinated between the two so that most major headings are identical. Both use automobiles, not cars or some other equivalent term. Under some circumstances a specialized library might apply LCSH headings for its main collection and use *Sears* for any small general area. Libraries can readily replace *Sears* with LCSH as their holdings grow. Both tools can be used inter-

SEARS

Drugs 615

   See also **Materia medica; Orphan drugs; Pharma-
      cology: Poisons and poisoning;** also classes of
      people with the subdivision *Drug use,* e.g.
      Criminals—Drug use; Youth—Drug use:
      etc.; and names of groups of drugs, e.g. **Nar-
      cotics;** etc.; and names of individual drugs
   x Pharmaceuticals
   xx **Chemistry, Medical and pharmaceutical; Mate-
      ria medica; Pharmacology; Pharmacy; Ther-
      apeutics**

Figure 9-1

LCSH

Drugs *(May Subd Geog)*
   ₍RM300-RM671 *(Pharmacology)*₎
   ₍RS *(Pharmacy)*₎
   BT Medical supplies
      Pharmacopoeias
      Therapeutics
   RT Chemistry, Pharmaceutical
      Chemotherapy
      Materia medica
      Pharmacology
      Pharmacy
   SA *headings beginning with the word* Drug; *also
      individual drugs and groups of drugs, e.g.*
      Narcotics, Stimulants; *also subdivision*
      Therapeutic use *under individual chem-
      icals and groups of chemicals, e.g.*
      Copper—Therapeutic use; Insulin—
      Therapeutic use; *and subdivision* Drug
      use *under names of individual persons
      and under classes of persons and ethnic
      groups*
   NT Anti-infective agents
      Antiallergic agents
      Antilipemic agents
      Botany, Medical
      Cardiovascular agents
      Contraceptive drugs

Dispensatories
Diuretics
Doping in sports
Drug utilization
Drugs—Administration
Drugs—Prescribing
Drugs, Nonprescription
Gynecologic drugs
Hypoglycemic agents
Immunosuppressive agents
Indandione
Magic and drugs
Medication errors
Medicine—Formulae,
   receipts, prescriptions
Orphan drugs
Parapsychology and drugs
Patent medicines
Pharmaceutical microbiology
Pharmaceutical policy
Pharmacognosy
Poisons
Prodrugs
Radiation-sensitizing
   agents
Respiratory agents
Synthetic drugs

Figure 9-2

changeably with DDC and LC classification, although *Sears* is
commonly associated with Dewey and LCSH with LC.

Compare the treatment of the heading ALCOHOLISM in LCSH (Figure 9-3) with that in *Sears* (Figure 9-4), noting that each indicates the
term is chiefly used for medical works. LCSH expands the topic area
considerably, providing a number of subdivisions as indicated by
dashes (ALCOHOLISM—PREVENTION) and combined terms (ALCO-
HOLISM AND CRIME).

Each list also provides a general classification number next to
major terms (some earlier editions of *Sears* omitted this, but it has
now been reinstated). Studying these numbers can aid in the
selection of subject headings by helping to place a particular heading

LCSH

Alcoholism *(May Subd Geog)*
  {HV5001-HV5720.5 (Social Pathology)},
  {RC564.7-RC565 (Medicine)},
  UF Addiction to alcohol
    Alcohol abuse
    Alcohol intoxication
    Dipsomania
    Drinking problem
    Drunkenness
    Inebriety
    Intemperance
    Intoxication
    Jellinek's disease
    Liquor problem
  BT Substance abuse
    Temperance
  RT Drinking of alcoholic beverages
  SA *subdivision* Alcohol use *under classes of per-*
      sons and ethnic groups; and under names
      of individual persons
  NT Alcoholics
    Astrology and alcoholism
    Korsakoff's syndrome
    Skid row
—**Complications and sequelae**
—**Diagnosis**
  NT Comprehensive Drinker Profile
—**Hospitals** *(May Subd Geog)*
  {RC564.73-RC564.75},
  UF Alcoholics—Hospitals and asylums
—**Physiological aspects**
  USE Alcohol—Physiological effect
—**Prevention**
——**Finance**
    NT Federal aid to alcoholism
          programs
—**Psychological aspects**
  UF Alcoholics—Psychology
—**Punched card systems**
  USE Punched card systems—Alcohol
—**Religious aspects**
  UF Alcoholism and religion
    Religion and alcoholism
——**Baptists, {Catholic Church, etc.}**
——**Buddhism, {Christianity, etc.}**
—**Study and teaching** *(May Subd Geog)*
  UF Alcohol education
    Alcoholism education
    Temperance—Study and teaching
——**Law and legislation**
    (May Subd Geog)
—**Treatment** *(May Subd Geog)*
  UF Keeley cure

  NT Alcoholism counseling
——**Finance**
    NT Federal aid to alcoholism
          programs
——**Law and legislation**
    (May Subd Geog)
Alcoholism and airplane accidents
  USE Drinking and airplane accidents
Alcoholism and crime *(May Subd Geog)*
  {HV5053-HV5055},
  Here are entered works on the relation between
alcoholism and criminal behavior or the incidence
of crime. Works on alcoholic intoxication as a
criminal offense or as a factor of criminal liability
are entered under the heading Drunkenness (Crim-
inal law)
  UF Crime and alcoholism
  BT Crime and criminals
  RT Drunkenness (Criminal law)
Alcoholism and employment
  (May Subd Geog)
  {HF5549.5.A4 (Personnel management)},
  UF Employment and alcoholism
  BT Personnel management
  RT Employee assistance programs
Alcoholism and religion
  USE Alcoholism—Religious aspects
Alcoholism and traffic accidents
  USE Drinking and traffic accidents
Alcoholism counseling *(May Subd Geog)*
  {HV5275-HV5283},
  BT Alcoholics—Rehabilitation
    Alcoholism—Treatment
    Counseling
    Health counseling
    Social service
  NT Alcoholism counselors
—**Law and legislation** *(May Subd Geog)*
Alcoholism counselors *(May Subd Geog)*
  UF Counselors, Alcoholism
  BT Alcoholism counseling
    Counselors
Alcoholism education
  USE Alcoholism—Study and teaching
Alcoholism in mass media *(May Subd Geog)*
  {P96.A42},
  BT Mass media
Alcoholism in pregnancy *(May Subd Geog)*
  {RG580.A},
  BT Drug abuse in pregnancy
    Obstetrical pharmacology
    Pregnancy, Complications of
  NT Fetal alcohol syndrome

Figure 9-3

SEARS
Alcoholism 616.86
> Use chiefly for medical materials, including works
> on drunkenness, dipsomania, etc.
> *See also* Alcohol—Physiological effect; Alcoholics;
> Drinking of alcoholic beverages; Temper-
> ance; also classes of people with the subdivi-
> sion *Alcohol use,* e.g. Youth—Alcohol use;
> etc.
> x Dipsomania; Drinking problem; Drunkenness; In-
> temperance; Intoxication; Liquor problem
> xx Alcohol; Drinking of alcoholic beverages;
> Drug abuse; Substance abuse; Temperance

Figure 9-4

in the general scheme of knowledge. For example, a *Sears* heading, such as DECISION MAKING, is rather vague, but the addition of three DDC numbers, 153.8, 302.3, and 658.4, indicates the heading can be used for materials in psychology, in ecology, and in general business management. When necessary, use the DDC numbers in *Sears* to aid the interpretation of the subject heading's meaning.

Both lists are arranged by the same general principles, but regardless of which is ultimately consulted, the introduction to *Sears*—"Principles of the *Sears List of Subject Headings*"—is essential reading for the beginner. Follow the same general process of assigning subject headings no matter which subject heading tool is employed. During the technical reading note the contents of the material by examining the Table of Contents, skimming all introductory material, and dipping into the text. Form a general idea of where the contents fit into the classification scheme. Establish a tentative notation and headings by consulting the cataloging tools. Then, if necessary, check the shelf list and the catalog before making a firm decision. After the call number is established and subject headings assigned, select the cross references to complete the process.

Using *Sears*

Sears, intended to be a working record, leaves one half of each page blank for the addition of such local topics and proper noun subjects as are assigned in individual libraries. Created for collections of less than 50,000 items, *Sears* provides terms in common American usage, rather than scientific or technical language. Space is saved by not listing every possible term, but by giving general permission to add certain categories of headings as needed. These include common names, such as flower or animal names, proper names and corporate bodies. (The preface to *Sears* provides a list of "Headings to be added by the cataloger.") When in doubt about the correct form to use for a name or corporate body, follow the rules in AACR2. Space is also saved by "Key" headings which serve as models for subdivision of proper names not listed:

presidents	Presidents—United States
authors	Shakespeare, William
peoples	Indians of North America
countries	United States
states	Ohio
municipalities	Chicago (Ill.)
language	English Language
literature	English Literature
wars	World War 1939–1945

Besides these, other general lists of subdivisions are provided in the preface and may be added to headings as needed, for example, SCIENCE—DICTIONARIES. These subdivisions are generally a form of publication such as maps, bibliographies, charts, encyclopedias, periodicals, etc.

When a subject heading is assigned from these general, unlisted categories, this decision must be recorded, just as when a decision is made about the form of a proper name. With *Sears*, however, no separate authority file is necessary, for the blank half of each page is intended for this purpose. Record the decision by writing the heading in proper alphabetical order, on the right-hand side of the page. Maintain these records carefully, for they make *Sears* a useful working tool for an individual collection.

First turn to a general term suggested by the content. Often help will appear at this point in the form of a scope note giving a general definition of the content appropriate for this heading.

Assigning
Headings in Sears

After the scope note are listed several *see also* headings, which are related and usually more specific. Consider whether any of these is more appropriate for the work being cataloged. If for example (in Figure 9-5) CHILDREN—COSTUME might be a more accurate heading, turn to that place and read the scope note to see if it is appropriate.

If a decision is made to stay with COSTUME, and if that heading has never been used in the catalog before, this decision is recorded by making a check mark against the heading.

The cataloger of course is not limited to the heading COSTUME because, at least in theory, any number of subject entries can be added for any one item. In practice, three specific subject headings are normally sufficient. Do not assign both a general and a specific subject heading for the same work. For example, FANS, HATS, and COSTUME should not be assigned to one item. Always be specific, and remember that in many cases a single subject heading can represent the entire contents of an item as accurately as is possible. Cross references can then be added to guide users to that term. It is

Costume 391

> Use for descriptive and historical materials on the costume of particular countries or periods and for materials on fancy costume and theatrical costumes. Materials dealing with clothing from a practical standpoint, including the art of dress, are entered under **Clothing and dress.** Materials describing the prevailing mode or style in dress are entered under **Fashion**

> *See also*

Arms and armor	**Hats**
Clothing and dress	**Makeup, Theatrical**
Cosmetics	**Millinery**
Fans	**Uniforms, Military**
Fashion	**Wigs**

> *also* classes of people with the subdivision *Costume,* e.g. **Children—Costume;** etc.
> x Acting—Costume; Fancy dress; Style in dress; Theatrical costume
> xx **Clothing and dress; Ethnology; Fashion; Manners and customs**

Children—Costume 391

> Use for descriptive and historical materials on children's costume among various nations and at different periods. Materials dealing with children's clothing from a practical standpoint are entered under **Children's clothing**

Figure 9-5

not obligatory to give each item a subject heading. If the content is vague and no specific subject can be found do not assign one.

Cross References

Because users may not think of the heading COSTUME when searching for this topic, but look for THEATRICAL COSTUME or FASHION instead, a network of cross references is built to help locate the correct heading. The decision to use the subject heading COSTUME is recorded in *Sears* and also added to the catalog record itself in the tracings. The record of the cross references created is, however, recorded only in *Sears*.

It is impossible to predict all the terms a user might think of trying, but *Sears* does provide the more obvious ones. Look at the single "x" term under COSTUME (Figure 9-5).

Single x terms are never used in the catalog as subject headings. They are rather terms related to the chosen subject heading and may be used to create *see* references. Make such references only when it is likely a user might look for a particular term. *See* references guide users from terms not used in the catalog to correct terms.

In Figure 9-6, a *see* reference has been created in the catalog for the term "Fancy dress." This action is recorded in *Sears* by checking the term as it appeared under COSTUME (Figure 9-7) and elsewhere in *Sears* as it appeared in the alphabetical sequence (Figure 9-8).

```
┌─────────────────────────────────────────────────────────┐
│                                                           │
│         Fancy dress                                       │
│                                                           │
│            see                                            │
│                                                           │
│         COSTUME                                           │
│                                                           │
└─────────────────────────────────────────────────────────┘
```

Figure 9-6

✔

x Acting—Costume; Fancy dress; Style in dress;
   Theatrical costume

Famines—United States 904
   x United States—Famines
✔ Fancy dress. *See* **Costume**
Fans 391
   xx **Costume**
Fantastic fiction 808.3; Fic
   See also **Science fiction**
   xx **Fiction**

Figure 9-7   Figure 9-8

Double "xx" terms appear in bold face type and are legitimate subject headings (Figure 9-5). They are normally more general in meaning or of more or less equal specificity. Users may think of subjects too general for their specific needs and a *see also* reference may be helpful to them. *See also* references refer the user from a more general term to one more specific. They should only be created when there is a known need (Figure 9-9).

```
┌─────────────────────────────────────────────────────────┐
│                                                           │
│         CLOTHING AND DRESS                                │
│                                                           │
│            see also                                       │
│                                                           │
│         COSTUME                                           │
│                                                           │
└─────────────────────────────────────────────────────────┘
```

Figure 9-9

Make a check mark in front of any "xx" term used (Figure 9-10). Then, to complete the record, turn to another page in *Sears* and check any *see also* references made under CLOTHING AND DRESS (Figure 9-11).

✔
See also **Children's clothing; Clothing and dress Costume; Dress accessories; Dressmaking; Fashion; Men's clothing; Tailoring; Women's** clothing; etc.; also names of articles of clothing and accessories, e.g. **Buttons; Hats; Hosiery; Leather garments; Shoes and shoe industry;** etc.

✔
xx **Clothing and dress; Ethnology; Fashion; Manners and customs**

Figure 9-10   Figure 9-11   111

```
CLOTHING AND DRESS

    see also

names of articles of clothing and
accessories e.g., BUTTONS
```

Figure 9-12

Sears also provides *see* and *see also* GENERAL REFERENCES that give blanket directions for all headings in a certain group (Figure 9-12).

Some catalogers prefer to create the cross reference authority file on cards, rather than checking a specific edition of *Sears*. In that case, type the card as the cross reference appears in the catalog and file alphabetically.

The decision to make a cross reference should be made carefully by each library, for after cross references are in place, it is difficult to know whether they are helping users or confusing them. Make only references that lead users to specific items in the collection. Once a network of references is in place in the catalog, it need never be replaced.

SPECIFIC SUBJECT AREAS

Assigning subject headings for language and literature, and geography and history, requires as much thought and attention as does classification in those areas. Dewey provides area tables for both language and literature and divides geography from history. History is shelved by periods. *Sears* provides language and literature models for assigning subject headings and divides geography and history in much the same way as Dewey.

Language and
Literature

When assigning subject headings in the areas of language and literature the emphasis is normally not on the subject of the content, but on the language and form. The *Sears* list reflects this by providing headings indicating whether a work is a Greek or Latin dictionary, an American play or a British novel. By using the subject heading ENGLISH LANGUAGE as a model the cataloger can assign headings for works dealing with various aspects of any language.

FRENCH LANGUAGE—DICTIONARIES
RUSSIAN LANGUAGE—HISTORY
JAPANESE LANGUAGE—PRONUNCIATION

It is important to know the language in which a work of literature is written, but here the situation is more complex. COLLECTIVE

WORKS may contain either works of literature or critical discussions of those works.

ENGLISH LITERATURE and its subdivisions serve as the model heading:

English literature 820
　Subdivisions used under this heading may be used under
　　other literatures.

Two subdivisions are especially useful. The one used for collective works:

ENGLISH LITERATURE—COLLECTIONS

and the one used for critical works:

ENGLISH LITERATURE—HISTORY AND CRITICISM

Use the entire subdivision HISTORY AND CRITICISM to identify criticism of a literary form, i.e., FRENCH DRAMA—HISTORY AND CRITICISM.

Assign no subject heading for works written by an individual author. The user searches either under the author's name, i.e., Miller, Arthur, or the title, *Death of a Salesman.* Added headings are unnecessary.

Assigning subject headings for fiction can be as confusing as providing a classification number. The heading FICTION is used only for works dealing with fiction as a literary form; HISTORICAL FICTION only for materials about historical fiction. SCIENCE FICTION, however, leads the user to science fiction novels. There is a heading SEA STORIES provided for fictional works dealing with the sea, but someone interested in reading a historical novel finds this form in the catalog by the circuitous route of locating a subject heading indicating a historical period—for example, U.S.—HISTORY—CIVIL WAR, 1861–1865—and checking to see if "Fiction" has been added as a subdivision. Fiction as a subdivision can be added to any subject heading when appropriate; e.g., OLD AGE—FICTION. However, many libraries choose to add no subject headings at all to fictional works, reasoning that patrons will use the catalog to find some titles, but frequently select materials by browsing. Some libraries try to facilitate browsing by creating separate sections for historical fiction or mystery stories. This method also has drawbacks, because it becomes more difficult to locate individual works when they are separated from the general fiction collection. Juvenile materials are much more likely to receive the subdivision —FICTION, since young reader's interests and school curricular interests bring requests for a story about the circus or one that takes place in a home state or particular historical period.

Another type of literature that may cause confusion in assigning subject headings is biography. Works discussing biography as a literary form are assigned the heading BIOGRAPHY (AS A LITERARY FORM). This will be a relatively small amount of material.

Works recounting the lives of people, either individually or collectively, are more numerous and in far greater demand. For the life of an individual the only subject heading absolutely necessary is the name of that person, inverted, and written in capitals at the top of the card: NIGHTINGALE, FLORENCE. If there is doubt about which form of the name to use, consult AACR2 or the name authority file and record the decision in *Sears*. The Library of Congress often assigns additional subject headings to biographical works and might add NURSES AND NURSING or GREAT BRITAIN—HISTORY—CRIMEAN WAR, 1853–1856 to a biography of Miss Nightingale. Normally this is not necessary. Make such headings only when a biography contains so much information about a field that it is also a useful reference for the topic. For example, a biography of Marie Antoinette could be assigned an additional subject heading, FRANCE—HISTORY—REVOLUTION—1789–1799. Do not do this as a matter of course, only when it is warranted by the contents.

Normally, the subdivision BIOGRAPHY is never used after an individual name, but there can be exceptions. When there is voluminous material about an individual, it is necessary to use subdivisions after the name. The model SHAKESPEARE, WILLIAM shows such examples: SHAKESPEARE, WILLIAM—BIBLIOGRAPHY; SHAKESPEARE, WILLIAM—ADAPTATIONS; or SHAKESPEARE, WILLIAM—BIOGRAPHY. Otherwise use BIOGRAPHY only as a subdivision for collective biographies—those works that contain biographies of more than three individuals. When these collective biographies are organized by place, the place may be the subject heading, subdivided by biography.

Title—Makers of Modern England
Subject heading—GREAT BRITAIN—BIOGRAPHY

When they are organized by class of person and there is no adequate term to describe its members, use the subject in general, subdivided by biography:

Title—Great Quarterbacks of the NFL
Subject heading—FOOTBALL—BIOGRAPHY

Otherwise, enter under terms such as

ARTISTS, SPIES, DICTATORS

and do not add the subdivision BIOGRAPHY.

The name of any geographical area or place—country, state, city, or other unit—may be used as a subject heading in *Sears*. These geographic units can be made more specific by adding subject subdivisions. Likewise, certain subjects, whose treatment is limited to a particular locality, can be made more specific by subdividing by geographical unit.

Dewey makes provisions for locating materials by place with the addition of an area notation, and when this option is employed, specific directions in the schedules are carefully followed. *Sears* also permits place to be added, and here too directions must be carefully observed. Unlike Dewey, *Sears* sometimes directs that place will come first, followed by subject. At other times subject is divided by place. If it is important to indicate place in a subject heading, consult *Sears* for the correct procedure.

Sometimes directions for adding place will be found with the subject headings, as illustrated in the following examples found in *Sears*:

Socialism (may subdiv. geog.) 320.5; 335

This is a general directive that this subject heading may be divided by any area unit the cataloger feels is necessary.

SOCIALISM—ITALY
SOCIALISM—MANCHESTER

In a similar general directive:

Reconstruction (1939–1951) (may subdiv. geog. except U.S.)
    940.53

the instruction means that the subject heading may be subdivided by any area unit *except* the United States. For example:

RECONSTRUCTION (1939–1951)—GREECE

Place is a common method of identification and *Sears* provides many examples. Any appropriate term may be subdivided by place even though no model exists. There are no definite rules to follow in such cases, but keep in mind whether the subject aspect or the place aspect is most important. Record all decisions in *Sears*.

On the library shelf, materials dealing with history are arranged chronologically by country. Subject headings indicating historical periods are also arranged chronologically in the catalog as indicated in the subject heading list (Figure 9-13).

Assign subject headings in the form prescribed. When the time period covered by the item does not coincide with the dates of the subject heading, use the time period that most closely corresponds rather than changing the dates given in *Sears*.

Geography and
History

History

115

United States—History—1783–1809 973.4
    See also **Lewis and Clark Expedition (1804–1806);**
        Louisiana Purchase; United States—Consti-
        tutional history
    x Confederation of American colonies
United States—History—1783–1865 973.5
United States—History—1801–1805, Tripolitan War
    973.4
    x Tripoline War
    xx **Pirates**
United States—History—1812–1815, War of 1812
    973.5
    x War of 1812
United States—History—1815–1861 973.5–973.6
    See also **Black Hawk War, 1832**
United States—1845–1848, War with Mexico 973.6
    x Mexican War, 1845–1848

Figure 9-13

Library of Congress Subject Headings

Published in three volumes, available and updated in microfiche, computer files, and monthly accumulation of *Weekly Lists*, the Library of Congress Subject Headings provide a more detailed authority file with more than 160,000 subject headings. Whereas *Sears* gives a suggested Dewey number, LCSH frequently lists the broad LC class number with the most common terms.

LCSH has abandoned the familiar *see* and *see also* notations to follow a cross reference code more commonly associated with lists used by thesauri for computerized bibliographic databases (Figure 9-14). Thesauri are created to aid the computer in creation of a *see* and *see also* network, and computers will play a larger role in subject access in the future.

Agricultural machinery *(May Subd Geog)*
    S671-S760,
    UF Agriculture—Equipment and supplies
        Crops—Machinery
        Farm machinery
    BT Farm supply industries
        Implements, utensils, etc.
        Tools
    RT Farm equipment
        Machine-tractor stations
    SA *subdivision* Machinery *under names of*
        crops, e.g. Corn—Machinery
    NT Agricultural engineering
        Agricultural implements
        Agricultural instruments
        Corn planters (Machines)
        Cotton planters (Machines)

Figure 9-14

UF = used for

Agricultural machinery is the term to be "used for," or instead of,

"UF terms" which will not be found as subject headings in the catalog.

BT = broader term

BTs have a broader meaning—tools, for example, would encompass agricultural machinery. If tools is an established heading in the catalog a *see also* heading could be created: "Tools—*see also* Agricultural machinery."

RT = related terms

These terms have some association other than hierarchy with agricultural machinery.

SA = *see also*

Here instructions are provided to aid in creating an entire group of headings. Rather than listing the names of all farm crops individually, permission is given to use the term machinery with the name of any crop.

NT = narrower term

Terms with a narrower meaning. Narrower terms can also serve as *see also* references—if they are already established in the catalog. If some materials are cataloged under agricultural instruments, a reference could be created that would read "agricultural machinery *see also* agricultural instruments."

The cataloger should consider the reference structure when assigning a subject heading, even if no cross references are to be created. BTs and NTs make it possible to consider headings easily, either more general or more specific than the ones being consulted, while related terms should also be considered as alternatives.

Beginning catalogers often assign headings that are too broad. These are of little use to the patron. If it is necessary when searching for information on canaries to look through hundreds of "birds" headings, it is probably more productive to browse the shelves. Always be as specific as possible for the convenience of the user.

Subject headings, like other access points, not only identify individual items, but should gather together items on the same topic. For example, CIVIL RIGHTS has a long list of related *see also* terms. However, all items about civil rights should share one, common subject heading. Patrons should not have to search under a number of related headings to find items on a single topic.

Assigning Subject Headings

117

Designing a useful *see* and *see also* structure will seem confusing to the beginner and, when purchased copy is relied on, it is easier to ignore such references. No one expects a catalog stuffed with every possible *see* and *see also*; but after a period of working with users most librarians quickly become aware when cross references will be helpful. Automation, by linking terms, makes it possible to send users to related terms they have not thought to look under. Remember, however, such a structure must first be created in the catalog.

Annotated Card Program

A subject heading list that especially focuses on materials intended for children is the AC Subject Headings for juvenile literature provided by the ANNOTATED CARD PROGRAM (AC), a service of the Library of Congress. Begun in 1965, the purpose of the program is to provide a more appropriate subject treatment for, and an easier subject access to, juvenile materials. An explanation of the program, as well as the list itself, can be found in LCSH. The AC list is to be used in conjunction with LCSH.

AC subject headings are found in brackets on Library of Congress printed cards that have an AC following the printed LC number. They are also identified in a field in a MARC record. They are thus easily distinguished from the regular LCSH terms also in the record. The cataloger selects the set of headings best suited to the age of the user of the local catalog.

There are several differences between AC and LC headings:

1. AC headings do not use subdivisions such as juvenile literature.

2. Subdivisions such as United States and American are rarely used as most materials in libraries for children and young people are assumed to be American in scope.

3. Geographic subdivision for subject headings denoting persons, such as actors or dancers, are omitted.

4. Subject headings are supplied for fiction when it will bring out the most important aspect of the work, i.e., Baseball–Fiction.

5. Popular, rather than scientific terms, are used, i.e., fossils rather than paleontology.

6. A general subject heading may be added to a specific one if it would be useful to the patrons: organic and paper crafts; toys and handicrafts.

The AC subject heading list is not intended as a stand-alone list. It offers an alternative to a library that prefers headings from the Library of Congress, but needs options for the children's collection. It is not a substitute for *Sears*.

SUMMARY

Classification locates items together on the shelf according to their subjects. Subject headings locate items by subject in the catalog, making it possible to bring out various facets of the subject of a work and to gather common topics under a standard term. To prevent the scattering of related materials, a controlled vocabulary is selected from a standard list. In the United States the two most common lists for general collections are *Sears List of Subject Headings* and *Library of Congress Subject Headings*. The lists are compatible and may be used together if necessary. General libraries with small collections usually prefer the shorter, simpler, and more general terms found in *Sears*.

A list of subject headings is really a network of subject entries and cross references containing general subjects, specific subjects, divisions of subjects, cross references from subjects not used, references from one subject to related subjects, and notes indicating the scope of a subject. To guide users through this network *see* references (from terms not used to terms used) and *see also* references (from one subject to another, related, one) are suggested in the list. An authority file should be kept to record all decisions about subject headings, and *Sears* leaves the right hand side of each page blank so that terms can be added as they are used.

The general topic of a work, determined during the technical reading, indicates where to begin to consult the subject list. Scope notes and references aid the selection of headings. The cataloger builds a consistent catalog by using a standard list and following directions carefully. Like items should be gathered together by using one specific heading.

CHAPTER REVIEW

Terms to understand:

Annotated Card Program (AC)   general reference
collective works   word-by-word filing

Assigning subject headings:

Determine the general subject or subjects by technical reading.
After the classification number has been decided, consult related subject headings in the list.
Select the most specific headings possible, normally limiting the number to three.
Assign the appropriate *see* and *see also* headings.

Subject headings—Literature:

Do not assign subject headings to single works of literature by one
author.

Follow the model provided for literature—ENGLISH LITERATURE
with its subdivisions.

For critical works about literature use the subdivision —HISTORY
AND CRITICISM.

Subject headings—Geography and history:

Do not subdivide by place without checking the proper subject
heading and the models for countries, states, cities, or other unit.

Observe the chronological arrangement of historical subject headings, fitting the content to the dates in the headings.

CHAPTER 10

CATALOGING WITH COPY

THE PROCESS of describing a work, choosing access points, and assigning a classification notation is referred to as ORIGINAL CATALOGING. Many items require original cataloging, including corporate reports, most K–12 textbooks, certain audio-visual materials, and locally printed or produced works. These are examples of the types of materials that the Library of Congress does not place in its collection and does not catalog; therefore, prepared copy is rarely available. Cataloging copy is available, however, for most trade books and government documents, and for some audio-visual materials. This copy can be found on the back of title pages, retrieved from BIBLIOGRAPHIC UTILITIES, or purchased from the Library of Congress, publishers, and jobbers. Many selection tools, such as the H. W. Wilson *Standard Catalog* series (which includes bibliographies for senior and junior high schools and public libraries as well as fiction and children's collections), give cataloging information. The *Booklist*, a periodical that lists a selection of new material in each issue, prints cataloging information, as does the *Weekly Record*, a weekly list of newly published American books.

Since cataloging copy is prepared according to whatever code is current at the time, it can vary widely from current practice in such details as subject headings, punctuation, and capitalization. Copy retrieved from a bibliographic database may conform to local practice, rather than national standards.

Some libraries use prepared copy without questioning its accuracy. Others carefully compare the copy with the item in hand, with the local catalog, and with current cataloging tools. At least make sure that the copy matches the work in hand because this cannot be taken for granted. Copy for different editions may differ considerably and sometimes mistakes in ordering occur. The extent to which catalog copy is checked and revised depends on the policies and working conditions of particular libraries. When many demands are placed on the librarian's time, editing catalog copy may take low priority. If the catalog is considered merely as a finding device for individual items, there is little reason to spend time integrating copy in order to standardize access. However, most libraries have open shelves where patrons search for and retrieve their own materials. They will be most successful when the catalog brings together works of individual authors, when subjects are found together, and when there is some consistency in access points. Likewise, library networking can succeed only if entries are standardized. And only if time is spent checking copy can such a catalog be created.

CATALOGING IN PUBLICATION

The most accessible catalog copy is the CATALOGING IN PUBLICATION (CIP) data found on the verso (back) of the title page of most trade books and many government publications (Figure 10-1). American publishers submit books in proof form to the CIP office at Library of Congress. Materials are cataloged as completely as possible from the proofs and the information sent to the publishers to include in the printed book.

CIP Record

Library of Congress Cataloging-in-Publication Data

```
Pilla, Marianne Laino, 1955—
    Resources for middle—grade reluctant readers.

    Bibliography: p. 96.
    Includes indexes.
    1.  High interest—low vocabulary books——Bibliography.
2. Slow learning children——Books and reading.
I. Title.
Z1039.S5P54  1987          016.37192'64          87—3736
ISBN 0—87287—547—4
```

Figure 10-1

Because the cataloger sees only the galley proof, which is unpaged and usually without illustrations, certain areas of description are omitted. These include other title information, the statement of responsibility, edition, publication, and physical description areas. When CIP data is used these areas must be added to complete the catalog record (Figure 10-2).

COMPLETED RECORD: LEVEL TWO

```
Pilla, Marianne Laino, 1955—
    Resources for middle—grade reluctant readers:
a guide for libraries / Marianne Laino Pilla. ——
Littleton, Colo. : Libraries Unlimited, c1987.
    125 p.

    Bibliography: p. 96.
    Includes indexes.
    ISBN 0—87287—547—4

    1. High interest—low vocabulary books——Bibliography.
2. Slow learning children——Books and reading. I. Title.
```

Figure 10-2

With the book in hand, it is a simple task for a clerk to complete the cataloging record. Using CIP data is more efficient than doing completely original cataloging. Access points, subject headings, classification number, and notes are all supplied, and the record need not be completed by a professional cataloger. A standard main entry has been selected. However, the information must still be converted into a catalog record, such as a typed or printed card, or electronic format.

When relying on CIP data the cataloger first decides which level of description is desired. In Figure 10-2, CIP data is used for Level Two description. Level One description would be formatted as shown in Figure 10-3 below.

COMPLETED RECORD: LEVEL ONE

```
Pilla, Marianne Laino, 1955-
    Resources for middle-grade reluctant readers. --
Libraries Unlimited, c1987.
    125 p.

    Bibliography: p. 96.
    Includes indexes.
    ISBN 0-87287-547-4

    1. Easy reading material--Bibliography. 2. Slow
learning children--Books and reading. I. Title.
```

Figure 10-3

Completing the description does not complete the cataloging record. Access points and a call number must still be assigned. Since CIP data provides a standard main entry, use as is. If there is a problem of conflict with the catalog, a cross reference can be used to resolve it. Recommended subject headings and added entries need examination. In Figure 10-1, two Library of Congress subject headings are suggested and subject cards may be prepared for both. Some libraries, using *Sears*, might change any headings not compatible with *Sears*, as illustrated in Figure 10-3. Added entries must be examined with the same care. The CIP data in Figure 10-1 lists only a title added entry, certainly essential for retrieval.

Finally, the cataloger provides a classification number. A library following LCC will normally assign the LCC number as is from CIP. Accepting the DDC number as is may lead to shelving problems.

The Dewey classification number on CIP copy is from the unabridged edition of the DDC in use when the material was cataloged. This may not be the edition of DDC that the library is using. If classification numbers are considered only as location devices this will not matter a great deal, but if the library is attempting to arrange its collection on the shelf in a logical sequence for the browser, the CIP number must be compared against the local shelf list.

Other considerations remain. Various options for arranging material using DDC were discussed in Chapter 8. Each library makes its own decisions about fiction, biography, critical works, and so forth. If the integrity of the shelving scheme is to be maintained, then the DDC number found on copy must be altered to conform to these local decisions.

For example, look at Figure 10-1, the first example of CIP copy. When this number is checked in Dewey, it is discovered that the library has two choices: to shelve all bibliographies together under 016 (subject bibliographies and catalogs) and add the class number to arrange by subject; or to arrange them with their appropriate subject, adding 016 to keep them together.

The CIP number would place this book in the bibliography section 016 near others dealing with special education (371.92'64). Equally correct would be 371.92'64'016, which would shelve the book in the special education for slow learners section; with the 016 assuring all bibliographies would rest together within that section.

CIP numbers, which are taken from the unabridged Dewey, often seem excessively long. However, PRIME MARKS indicate where the numbers can be shortened without destroying the meaning of the notation. A library using the abridged edition usually finds the shortened number fits into its scheme. However, this isn't true when number building has been done. For example, the abridged Dewey offers a similiar option for bibliographies, but if the book is to be placed with special education rather than bibliographies it will be necessary to consult the tables to arrive at the correct abridged number 371.92016.

Finally, as shown in Chapter 8, the Dewey number is completed with the addition of a book or Cutter number.

Because converting the CIP data into the final catalog entry can be a time-consuming project, many libraries prefer to purchase printed cards and use CIP data, if at all, only to create a temporary record in the catalog.

PURCHASED COPY

Many school, public, and academic libraries purchase catalog cards from the Library of Congress. These are ordered in sets, using the LC order number printed on the verso of the title page, in CIP data, in many review sources, and on the LC card itself in the lower righthand corner. The cards arrive with tracings at the bottom, but without subject headings, added entries, or call numbers in place, all of which are typed in at the local library.

The body of the card (the description), normally Level Two, need not be altered; otherwise adapt the set to fit the collection. LC cards can reflect many cataloging codes, as well as different editions of subject headings. The library may wish to omit some subject headings or certain added entries. Simply cross them out of the tracing. If it is necessary to add or edit access points or subject headings, be sure to record the decision in the tracings. Suggested call numbers are printed at the bottom of LC cards, but the library can assign any call number.

Figure 10-4 shows an example of a Library of Congress card, cataloged with tools from an earlier decade. A library that receives this card faces several decisions.

This record has been completed with three subject headings and six added entries. In a special collection of Southern history, such thorough cataloging might be desirable. The local library should use only those headings likely to help the patron find a specific item. In a general collection, one subject heading for Wayne Co., N.C., would be adequate, and six added entries for editors, commissions, and a newspaper would be questioned. However, the librarian would still have to decide whether to update the subject headings.

Today many libraries receive cataloging copy from shared cataloging networks called bibliographic utilities. These utilities store millions of machine-readable cataloging records supplied by both Library of Congress and cooperating libraries of the network. OCLC (Online Computer Library Center), a familiar utility, in operation since 1967, is the largest of these services. Other utilities include RLIN (Research Libraries Information Network), WLN (Washington Library Network), and UTLAS (University of Toronto Library Automation System).

```
History of Wayne County, North Carolina : a collection of
    historical stories created by the Heritage Committee on the
    Bicentennial Commission and published in Goldsboro News-argus,
    April 6, 1975-July 4, 1976 / Bob Johnson and Charles S.
    Norwood, editors.--Goldsboro, N.C. : Wayne County Historical
    Association, 1979.
        x, 239 p., [3] leaves of plates : ill. ; cm.
        Title on spine: Wayne County history.
        ''Republished with additions.''
        1. Wayne Co., N.C.--History--Addresses, lectures. 2. Wayne
Co., N.C.--Biography--Addresses, essays, lectures. 3. Wayne
Co., N.C.--Genealogy-Addresses, essays, lectures. I. Johnson,
Bob, 1935- II. Norwood, Charles S., 1904- III. Bicentennial
Commission, Goldsboro, N.C. Heritage Committee. IV. News-argus,
Goldsboro, N.C. V. Wayne County Historical Association.
VI. Title : Wayne County history.
    F262.W4H57          975-6'395              79-126431
                        80                     MARC
```

Figure 10-4

The growth of these networks has been possible because of the development of the MARC format. In the mid-1960s, the Library of Congress began distributing machine-readable cataloging (MARC). At first, sixteen selected libraries received these tapes containing the bibliographic records of books cataloged at the Library of Congress. These libraries tested and experimented with the MARC format, which was soon greatly expanded and revised. In 1969, the MARC Distribution Service began. For an annual fee the subscriber receives each week a magnetic tape containing cataloging done at the Library during the previous week. Although the number of subscribers has been limited, many libraries have benefited. Jobbers, bibliographic utilities, and other suppliers of cataloging data subscribe to MARC tapes and use them to provide thousands of libraries with standard cataloging copy. Today, many other libraries besides the Library of Congress are able to share machine-readable cataloging records.

Libraries belonging to a bibliographic utility can search a database for cataloging records, or add unique records of their own for others to share. They can receive records on printed cards or on magnetic tapes. Libraries may edit or reformat the MARC record according to their own requirements. The same limits, however, of time, staff, and working conditions still apply when cataloging with MARC records, and some libraries will modify a MARC record very little.

Bibliographic utilities also contain many older records; however, since the database can be manipulated electronically it is easier to update these records than the LC card stock. Compare the subject headings retrieved from the OCLC database (Figure 10-5) to those received in the purchased copy (Figure 10-4).

```
▶13 651  0   Wayne County (N.C.) ⧧× History.
▶14 651  0   Wayne County (N.C.) ⧧× Biography.
▶15 651  0   Wayne County (N.C.) ⧧× Genealogy.
▶16 700 10   Johnson, Bob, ⧧d 1935- ⧧w cn ¶
```

Figure 10-5

Figure 10-6 illustrates the description of a book cataloged by the Annotated Card Program (AC cataloging always adds an annotation in the notes area). Two sets of subject headings were added in the tracings. The AC headings were identified by brackets. The choice of subject headings depends on the catalog's clientele. In a catalog that

```
Quackenbush, Robert M.
    Don't you dare shoot that bear! a story of
Theodore Roosevelt. / Robert Quackenbush. --
Englewood Cliffs, N.J. : Prentice-Hall, c1984.
    36 p. : col. ill. ; 24 cm.

    A humorous biography of the twenty-sixth
president, emphasizing his love of animals and
wildlife and his activities as a conservationist.

LC Subject Headings

    1. Roosevelt, Theodore, 1858-1919--Juvenile literature
2. Presidents, United States, Biography--Juvenile
literature.  3. Conservation of natural resources--
United States--History--Juvenile literature.

AC Subject Headings

    [1. Roosevelt, Theodore, 1858-1919.  2. Presidents
3. Conservationists.  4. Conservation of natural
resources.]
```

Figure 10-6   AC

serves both adults and young people, juvenile items need to be identified. In a school or children's collection it is unnecessary to label everything in this way. AC headings are usually simpler and omit place according to AC rules. Simply cross out the subject headings not used.

Whatever the source of cataloging copy, the catalog is a more useful tool when access points, subject headings, and classification are integrated into the existing catalog, gathering together the works of one author, the editions of one work, and material dealing with the same or similar subjects.

CATALOGING PROFILES

It is possible, because of the flexibility of the MARC format, to purchase copy that is designed for the use of a particular library. Bibliographic utilities, commercial vendors, state and regional processing centers, or others can provide customized cataloging. However, a CATALOGING PROFILE must first be developed by the local library. The following is an example of a jobber's specification form with both standard and alternate choices (Figure 10-7). These are filed once, providing permanent specifications, unless the library requests changes.

CATALOGING SPECIFICATIONS

Please check the standard or alternate specifications you desire for each of the categories listed below. Where you specify an alternate, it will be supplied without additional charge.

CATEGORY	STANDARD	ALTERNATES supplied without additional charge
5 **CATALOG CARDS, ALL BOOK CATEGORIES** H	☐ Headed and numbered catalog cards.	☐ Unheaded and unnumbered catalog cards. Book card and book pocket complete with author and title, call number omitted. Blank spine label, loose. ☐ Headed and unnumbered catalog cards. Book card and book pocket complete with author and title, call number omitted. Blank spine label, loose. NOTE: If you have checked either alternate above, do not check Categories 9 through 13.

Figure 10-7

This jobber supplies catalog cards with printed headings (subject headings and added entries) and call numbers as a standard service. However, on the right are listed those options available to libraries that wish to supply their own headings and/or call numbers.

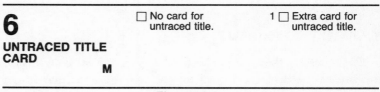

6 **UNTRACED TITLE CARD** M	☐ No card for untraced title.	1 ☐ Extra card for untraced title.

Figure 10-8

Some items, especially textbooks, may have titles that are considered non-distinctive, for example *Arithmetic*, *Basic Chemistry*, *Spanish One*. Many libraries do not trace, that is, do not create an entry for such titles, reasoning that they are practically useless for retrieval purposes. Collections that house few texts, or contain only texts, and institutions that divide their catalogs find title entry useful (see Figure 10-8).

A unit set will contain a card for every entry, and a card for the shelf list. Some libraries want to create additional entries, and keep other files. One or two extra main entry cards are therefore useful (see Figure 10-9).

7

**MAIN ENTRY
CARDS**

N

☐ No extra main entry
cards.

1 ☐ One extra main
entry card.

2 ☐ Two extra main
entry cards.

Figure 10-9

Public libraries often have one catalog for their entire collection. In order to aid their users in selecting materials, those items intended for children and young people are identified with a "J" in front of the call number. Such a designation makes little sense in a library or media center whose entire collection is intended for juveniles.

By selecting the standard choice in Figure 10-10, subject headings will normally have —JUVENILE LITERATURE attached.

8

JUVENILE

J

☐ No special
identification for
children's books.
Library of Congress
subject headings.

1 ☐ Fiction: Upper case "J" above author or call
number as chosen in Fiction specification
below. Non-Fiction (incl. Biography): Lower
case "j" before call number.

2 ☐ Trace children's subject headings on subject
added entry cards.

3 ☐ Fiction: Upper case "J" above author or call
number as chosen in Fiction specification
below. Non-Fiction (incl. Biography): Lower
case "j" before call number. In addition, trace
children's subject headings on subject added
entry cards.

Figure 10-10

By selecting #1, items intended for children and young people are identified with a J in the call number.

By selecting #2, a library will receive AC subject headings.

Selection #3 is a combination of both #1 and #2; therefore, juvenile materials would be identified on the shelf with a J, but in the catalog will have AC subject headings.

Selection #1 would commonly be used in a public library with one catalog for the entire collection.

Selection #2 would commonly be used in a library or media center whose entire collection is intended for juvenile users.

Selection #3 would commonly be used by a library with a separate juvenile department and a separate juvenile catalog.

129

9

FICTION

☐ F with first three letters of author's surname.	1 ☐ F with first two letters of author's surname.	A ☐ First letter of author's surname only.
	2 ☐ F with first letter of author's surname.	B ☐ No call number.
	3 ☐ F only.	*C ☐ Dewey number if given on MARC tape, with first three letters of author's surname.
	4 ☐ FIC with first three letters of author's surname.	
	5 ☐ FIC with first two letters of author's surname.	*D ☐ Dewey number if given on MARC tape, with first two letters of author's surname.
	6 ☐ FIC with first letter of author's surname.	*E ☐ Dewey number if given on MARC tape, with first letter of author's surname.
	7 ☐ FIC only.	
	8 ☐ First three letters of author's surname only.	*F ☐ Dewey number only, if given on MARC tape.
	9 ☐ First two letters of author's surname only.	*If no Dewey number is given, no call number will appear on components.

B

Figure 10-11

There are options for fiction as discussed in Chapter 8, and these are illustrated by the number of choices offered (see Figure 10-11). Some allow the library to add its own Cutter number; others supply letters for the author. A Dewey number is available if the Library of Congress has assigned one and recorded it on MARC tape.

CATEGORY	STANDARD	ALTERNATES supplied without additional charge	
10 **NON-FICTION**	☐ Dewey number with first letter of author's surname.	1 ☐ Dewey number with first two letters of author's surname.	3 ☐ Dewey number only.
			4 ☐ No call number.
		2 ☐ Dewey number with first three letters of author's surname.	

C

Figure 10-12

If the call number is regarded strictly as a finding device a library will accept a Dewey number as given, with or without letters of the author's surname, depending on whether a Cutter number is used (see Figure 10-12). Otherwise the option of no call number is selected and the library will add its own.

11

INDIVIDUAL BIOGRAPHY

☐ B with biographee's surname.

1 ☐ B with first three letters of biographee's surname.

2 ☐ B with first two letters of biographee's surname.

3 ☐ B with first letter of biographee's surname.

4 ☐ B.

5 ☐ 92 with biographee's surname.

6 ☐ 92 with first three letters of biographee's surname.

7 ☐ 92 with first two letters of biographee's surname.

8 ☐ 92 with first letter of biographee's surname.

9 ☐ 92.

A ☐ 921 with biographee's surname.

B ☐ 921 with first three letters of biographee's surname.

C ☐ 921 with first two letters of biographee's surname.

D ☐ 921 with first letter of biographee's surname.

E ☐ 921.

F ☐ No call number.

G ☐ Dewey number as given on MARC tape, with biographee's surname.

H ☐ Dewey number as given on MARC tape, with first three letters of biographee's surname.

I ☐ Dewey number as given on MARC tape, with first two letters of biographee's surname.

J ☐ Dewey number as given on MARC tape, with first letter of biographee's surname.

K ☐ Dewey number only.

D

Figure 10-13

There are options for biography, as discussed in Chapter 8, and these are illustrated by the number of choices offered (see Figures 10-13 and 10-14). Some allow the library to add its own Cutter number; others supply letters for the biographee or collective author. A Dewey number is available if Library of Congress has assigned one and recorded it on the MARC tape.

School and public libraries often indicate EASY BOOKS (mainly picture books intended primarily for young children) with an E rather

12
COLLECTIVE BIOGRAPHY

☐ 920 with first letter of author's surname.

1 ☐ 920 with first two letters of author's surname.

2 ☐ 920 with first three letters of author's surname.

3 ☐ 920.

4 ☐ 92 with first letter of author's surname.

5 ☐ 92 with first two letters of author's surname.

6 ☐ 92 with first three letters of author's surname.

7 ☐ 92.

8 ☐ No call number.

9 ☐ Dewey number as given on MARC tape, with first letter of author's surname.

A ☐ Dewey number as given on MARC tape, with first two letters of author's surname.

B ☐ Dewey number as given on MARC tape, with first three letters of author's surname.

C ☐ Dewey number only.

E

Figure 10-14

13
EASY BOOKS

☐ E with first letter of author's surname.

1 ☐ E with first two letters of author's surname.

2 ☐ E with first three letters of author's surname.

3 ☐ E.

4 ☐ Call numbers same as checked under FICTION category above.

5 ☐ No call number.

*6 ☐ Dewey number if given on MARC tape, with first letter of author's surname.

*7 ☐ Dewey number if given on MARC tape, with first two letters of author's surname.

*8 ☐ Dewey number if given on MARC tape, with the first three letters of author's surname.

*9 ☐ Dewey number only, if given on MARC tape.

*If no Dewey number is given, no call number will appear on components.

F

Figure 10-15

than a classification number, to provide a special collection for young users (see Figure 10-15). All E books will then be filed together, perhaps by author, perhaps in no particular order. Some libraries may prefer to shelve easy books with the rest of the collection and can order Dewey numbers if they have been assigned by the Library of Congress.

A jobber provides more than cataloging copy, and Figure 10-16 illustrates some of the processing options available.

PROCESSING SPECIFICATIONS

CATEGORY	STANDARD	ALTERNATES supplied without additional charge	
14 **MYLAR JACKET** JA	☐ Attached to book (dust jacket, when available, inserted into sized Mylar jacket and attached to book)	1 ☐ No Mylar jacket.	2 ☐ Mylar jacket, unfastened.
15 **BOOK POCKET &** **BOOK CARD** PO	☐ Complete with author, title, and call number, attached to back flyleaf.	1 ☐ Attached to front flyleaf.	2 ☐ Unfastened.
16 **SPINE LABEL** LA	☐ Complete with call number, attached to spine of book (or dust jacket when available) with bottom of label two inches from bottom of book.	1 ☐ Blank, unfastened. 2 ☐ Printed, unfastened.	3 ☐ Printed, attached to book (never on dust jacket).

ADDITIONAL OPTIONS

17 **POCKET LABELS**	☐ Unattached. Complete with library name and address, list price, and date of purchase	1 ☐ Attached.	
18 **THEFT-** **DETECTION** **DEVICES**		3M Tattle-Tape Book Detection System: 1 ☐ Type DS— sensitized/ desensitized— single adhesive to be inserted in book spine. 2 ☐ Type DS— sensitized/ desensitized— double adhesive to be inserted between pages in the gutter of the book. Checkpoint: 3 ☐ Single adhesive— applied behind book pocket. Please indicate the appropriate Checkpoint tag for your system: 3a ☐ Check label 23	3b ☐ Check label 28 3c ☐ Check label 31 3d ☐ Teeny beeper 34 3e ☐ Teeny beeper 37 3f ☐ Sticker 49 3g ☐ Sticker 50 3M Echo Tags 4 ☐ Single adhesive— applied behind book pocket
19 **INSTALLED** **COVER-UPS** ®	☐ No Cover-ups on paperbacks.	1 ☐ Install Cover-ups on all paperbacks. 2 ☐ Install Cover-ups as indicated on order.	Protect your paperback covers beneath a 15-mil thickness of clear plastic, permanently adhered to the cover. Installed Cover-Ups® are available for processed or unprocessed paperbacks at only $1.65 per book, regardless of size.

Figure 10-16

SUMMARY

Cataloging copy can be found in many sources, including the CIP data in most trade books, bibliographies that are used to select materials, and cards prepared by publishers, producers, or jobbers. The busy librarian may be tempted to use this copy as is, although it may not meet current cataloging practices or be accurate for the item in hand. Editions can vary for books of the same title from the same publisher; perhaps only portions of a multi-media kit have been purchased, or portions of an item may be missing. Similar problems arise when libraries use cataloging copy from a bibliographic utility. Copy retrieved must always match the item in hand. When users select materials from the catalog, any details that might affect their success should certainly be edited.

When description matches the item in hand, it should be used as is. When necessary, modify other parts of copy, whether CIP or prepared cards. Certain access points may be unnecessary in a particular collection, or, more rarely, additional access points should be added. *Sears* headings may be preferred or Library of Congress subject headings may be updated.

If a library strives to shelve like materials together, then Dewey numbers may need modification from those suggested. If cataloging is purchased from a jobber or a vendor, it is often possible to plan a cataloging profile that meets the needs of a particular institution. Whether cataloging is retrieved from CIP, a database, a publisher, or an LC card, editing the copy produces more accurate records.

CHAPTER REVIEW

Terms to understand:

bibliographic utilities	easy books
Cataloging in Publication (CIP)	original cataloging
cataloging profile	prime marks

Finding cataloging copy:

In selection sources such as *Standard Catalog*, or a bibliographic tool such as *Weekly Record*.
On verso of title page (CIP).
On purchased cards from LC.
On MARC tapes from LC.
On cards from jobbers and publishers.
On cataloging data from bibliographic utilities.

Using catalog copy:

Match to item in hand.
Use description as is when matched.
Check DDC number so similar subjects will be placed together.
Mark out unwanted access points.
Check the subject headings.

CHAPTER 11

BEHIND THE WORKROOM DOOR

THE NUMBER of typing, filing, processing, and record-keeping chores that must be done at the local library has decreased in the last decade. Cooperative and commercial processing centers have become so well-established that even the smallest library can routinely order materials cataloged, ready to be shelved. The consolidation of library systems and school districts has meant that a number of library records are now handled by a central office, and in many libraries a computer has taken over certain routine tasks such as keeping records and filing entries. However, there are always some chores that only the individual library can do for itself and these will vary from institution to institution.

Some small libraries may be legally required to keep as many records as a large institution without having the same number of support staff. Special libraries that collect only inhouse materials, reports, bulletins, videotapes and newsletters will probably be responsible for all processing and cataloging. Gifts are often handled by individual libraries, as are some audiovisual formats. Local records must be maintained for serials. Commercial services do not provide ANALYTICS or references to contents or materials, nor do they help maintain a catalog. Many of these tasks may be done by clerks and volunteers, but the librarian should develop simple and effective procedures for guiding their work. If date due slips fall out before items can be returned, if spine or bar code labels slide off before shelving, if catalog cards are rarely or improperly filed, or if computer files are not regularly updated, a library cannot run efficiently. No matter what the level of automation or centralization, no library can lock the workroom door permanently.

TRACKING MATERIALS

Accession Numbers and Shelf Lists

A nation attempts to keep track of its citizens with records; with birth and death certificates, and with individual designators such as social security numbers. Librarians keep control of materials in the collection in much the same manner. In order to keep records accurately, each item is assigned a unique number. This is usually an accession number, but could be a call number (see Chapter 8) or another designator. This may be stamped on the item with an automatic stamping machine, or the materials may be given codes.

The numbers may run in a sequence, starting with a number one for the first item acquired, and so on; or a break can be made by incorporating the year into the number. The first work received in 1988 would be given the number 88–0001; the second, 88–0002, proceeding through the year. Accession numbers thus provide a running account of numbers of materials acquired. Some libraries assign each format a different series of accession numbers, but this is confusing, almost impossible with the proliferation of formats, and not recommended. Whichever method is followed, each record should have a unique number.

Accession numbers are not always used. When DUPLICATES of an item are acquired, it is necessary to mark both the shelf list and the items with a copy number: copy 1, copy 2, and so forth. Copy numbers can also be added to the call number. Because duplicate items may be acquired after long intervals, or may be replacements, it is difficult to keep accurate records in this way. The practice does not supply items with a unique number and it is not recommended.

To assist in keeping an inventory, individual accession numbers are recorded on the shelf list card, providing a record of every item in the collection, while the catalog provides only the bibliographic record. Although the catalog does not normally reveal how many copies of an individual title are owned, the shelf list does supply this information. When an item is withdrawn from the collection, the accession number is deleted. Instead of one shelf list card for one title with all accession numbers, a separate shelf list can be provided for each item. This makes adding and deleting duplicates a simpler process because it does not involve pulling the shelf list card and erasing or typing in a number each time a copy is removed or added.

Accession numbers that have been retired should never be reused. If the item has been lost or stolen it may well reappear. Reuse of numbers also removes any value the accession number may have for statistical purposes.

Record on the shelf list card standard unique numbers such as International Standard Book Numbers (ISBN), Library of Congress card numbers (LCCN), International Standard Serial Numbers (ISSN), and Superintendent of Documents numbers. The shelf list should also include any unique numbers required for the library's computer management identification. Though the usefulness of recording these numbers is not always immediately apparent, when a library prepares to automate, it finds these numbers essential for locating machine-readable records.

With automation many librarians have abandoned the shelf list, relying on computer printouts as backups to the database. However, the printout lists only items currently entered; there is no record of strayed or stolen materials. Maintaining the shelf list as a backup provides an institutional memory bank to answer those questions that frequently arise when missing items reappear or must be replaced. The shelf list also provides a convenient authority file for those who do cataloging without easy access to the computer terminal. If a shelf list card can be easily reproduced with an automated system the shelf list should be retained. If not, the time involved in typing the card must be weighed against the usefulness of the shelf list. No computer backup is totally secure. At least a manual shelf list does not disappear when the computer starts crunching files.

Additional information recorded on the shelf list card depends on library policy. Some libraries record price in order to charge clients who lose items. Libraries that routinely charge prices from *Books in Print*, or charge a uniform fee according to each category of materials, need not record it.

STATISTICS

Statistical information may be divided into two types: that which shows the amount of work done, and that which records the holdings of the library. Statistics should be kept only to the extent they supply useful information; for example, those titles in each format, and sometimes in each category, that have been added or subtracted. Circulation figures are sometimes regarded as an indication of work done, and many libraries are legally required to report circulation figures, although they have little to do with services provided. It is difficult to judge which statistics are useful and which are not. Many libraries routinely report on numbers of new titles added, but even that number means little unless it is interpreted. For instance, how does the figure compare with acquisitions of libraries of similar size, with that of a year ago, or a decade ago, and what do these comparisons signify?

When records are kept by computer, statistics are more easily generated than when all counting is done manually. When a circulation and reserve system is automated, it is possible to keep records not only of how many times an item circulated, but also of how many times that item was requested and unavailable—an even more useful statistic for selection purposes. A librarian with little time to keep statistics, and even less time to interpret them, keeps statistical reports to a minimum and compiles them only when they serve a useful purpose.

INVENTORY

Like businesses, libraries take regular stock of their inventory. Some libraries take this process so seriously that they close the collection annually and track down every leaflet. Others never take formal inventory but manage equally well. The process of inventory-taking is not difficult. The materials on the shelves are simply compared to the shelf list, which may be done either manually or with an automated process. First any special collections that contain items that have been removed from their classified position are broken up and reshelved in their proper shelf list order. When the shelf list is checked against all the materials being circulated, the inventory is completed by recording the necessary information on those shelf list cards that show missing material. Some time later decisions can be made about replacement or withdrawal.

Inventory-taking is an expense of time, and there is little justification for its routine occurrence. If shelves are read frequently and accurately, and losses are few, inventories should be rare. Instead of taking a thorough inventory, in which time is wasted counting items that rarely circulate, some libraries spot-check popular or expensive areas such as the reference collection to get an indication of loss. If accurate records of additions and replacements are kept, it should not be necessary to take inventory routinely to arrive at a more or less correct count of items. After all, inventories can become incorrect seconds after they are completed. There is an old library saying, "If you don't miss it, you didn't need it," which contains a lot of truth. For those items that have never been missed, that no patron has ever inquired about, or conversely, that have never left the shelf, money and time spent on inventory-taking are wasted.

There are times when it is necessary to inventory. When a collection is to be broken up, or moved to a new location, it makes sense. If, because of losses, some kind of detection system is put in place, inventory should be taken before and after the system is installed. A change in format of catalog, from card to online, for example, would surely create a need for an inventory. But normally, lack of access by users, and amount of time spent by staff, cannot justify routine inventories.

CATALOG MAINTENANCE

Card catalogs require time-consuming attention: filing cards, shifting as drawers fill, providing guide cards and outside labels. All cards in the tracing need to be removed when an item is withdrawn, and any revision in call number or access points requires removing and replacing cards. Drawers should never be packed too tightly; three-quarters-full is the limit. Include guide cards to break up the alphabet for the convenience of users. Guide cards can indicate classification number and/or topics and should appear approximately every hundred cards.

A catalog created of machine-readable records also requires maintenance. Records need to be added to the database as new materials are acquired, and removed as materials are discarded or lost. Discrepancies occur with changes in cataloging rules and subject heading terminology. Simple mistakes crop up due to input errors. The shelf list needs to be maintained as a backup, and disk or tape back-up copies should be made frequently. For security store these in a safe place.

CIRCULATION

All libraries that lend materials must keep records, but some libraries need to know more than others. For example, a large public library may want to know who has an item only when the item becomes overdue, whereas most academic libraries want to be able to locate materials at any time. Computer circulation systems are a familiar sight in both large and small libraries, and microcomputer circulation programs are readily available. Before any circulation system is developed, whether manual or automated, a library should think carefully about the circulation information necessary for its operation. For instance, is it necessary to know what each borrower has currently? It probably is in any system such as a school, college, or business library, where it is necessary to withdraw the names of those who are no longer entitled to use the collection. School librarians could face the prospect of searching through several thousand cards to find out if a withdrawing student has outstanding materials. Filing behind a user I.D. number provides such information, but makes it more difficult to keep up with overdue materials.

Is it necessary to know where each individual item is from the moment it is checked out? Again it depends. Academic, school, or special libraries often have a policy of calling in material when others have need of it. These libraries make an effort to keep such a record for each item. Public libraries, however, will not usually notify a user to bring in materials unless they are overdue, and are usually only interested in knowing about an item when it is not returned on time. The kind of circulation records to keep and their complexity depend on what a library needs to know. Each added bit of information requires the creation of a file that has to be maintained, requiring time, effort, and budget resources. This is equally true for all library records. Records commonly kept in circulation files include authorized borrowers, charging procedures, discharging procedures, overdue control, reserve collections, and statistical reporting. However these functions are organized, the library should be able to define their purposes clearly and logically.

SERIALS

Many readers identify serials with PERIODICALS, but SERIALS can also include newspapers, yearbooks, proceedings, bulletins, in fact, any publication issued in parts and intended to be continued indefinitely. Many people who never think of reading a book depend on periodicals for information and serials are an important part of library collections, often accounting for the major portion of the budget for new materials.

Although the general principles for cataloging books also apply to these materials, there are several differences, and many libraries do not include them in the catalog. But whether cataloged or not, serial records must be kept, and their very nature can create problems. For most library items, once ordered, processed, and shelved, the record keeping is complete until the item is withdrawn. Not so with serials, especially periodicals. Because they are issued in parts, record keeping is a continuing process. Libraries regard it as a serious business when periodicals are missing from the collection, for they are expensive to order in terms both of money and time, and they are popular items. It is reasonable, therefore, to spend some time and thought on developing an efficient system of serials control.

Users want to know which serial titles are in a library, and whether any issues are missing. Librarians also want to be sure that they are getting what they paid for, and that the latest issue due has arrived. Records must be kept to answer these questions.

Serial orders are placed in different ways. Many systems annually place orders with jobbers, and normally all the librarian does is indicate titles to be added or deleted. If a library receives only a few titles, orders are probably placed with individual publishers. No matter how ordered, all serials, periodicals, and newspapers should be checked in on arrival. If this is not done efficiently, titles are lost, users are frustrated, and the library wastes money.

Periodicals and newspapers are checked in by title. Check-in forms can be purchased for different types of serials. These provide places to record the name of the publication and to check each issue in by date. The form should be typed at the same time the order is placed so there is no confusion about the title. It can also serve as the record for the user, and be stored as a page in a notebook, in a card file, in a VISIBLE FILE, or in a computer file. Besides title and issues received, other information can also be recorded, such as purchasing source and binding information. Serials frequently change titles. When this occurs simply start a new record and place a note to that effect on the old one. When periodicals and newspapers do not appear it is necessary to notify the publisher or jobber as soon as possible to assure service. This process is called CLAIMING. Some systems will claim all periodicals centrally; in others each library is responsible. Claims that are not filed promptly may not be honored by publishers.

If serial records are entered in the main catalog, follow regular rules. Identify the Chief Source of Information (Figure 4-2) and enter under either title or author. For serials, indicate on the catalog record not only what titles are available, but which issues or parts are owned by the library. Record this information in the NUMERIC AREA along with ALPHABETIC or CHRONOLOGICAL DESIGNATIONS immediately after the edition statement. This area is unique to serials. The numeric is frequently recorded directly after the title since edition information and statements of responsibility are rarely given for periodicals. Record the designation of the first issue in the library collection.

Online -- Vol. 1, No. 1 -

If the first issue is also identified by a date, give the numbering before the date.

Online -- Vol. 1, No. 1 (Jan. 1977) -

Occasionally a serial will be identified only by a date. In that case, simply add the date in this area.

NSTA Report -- Oct./Nov. 1988 -

Since at this point there is no way of knowing how long the serial will be issued or received by the library, the entry is left "open," indicated by the dash. This OPEN ENTRY is closed when the last issue arrives.

Online -- Vol. 1, No. 1 (Jan. 1977) -
Vol. 4, No. 12 (Dec. 1980)

Serials frequently change titles; when this occurs supply a reference card to tie the titles together, and begin cataloging under the new title.

Some serials, such as annuals and yearbooks (e.g., *Yearbook of Agriculture*), are issued with individual titles and deal with a variety of topics. Libraries may catalog these as serials, but it is usually more practicable to separate, catalog, and classify them as single works, providing an added entry for the serials title.

Serials in periodical form are important reference sources and are often stored as a permanent part of the collection instead of being discarded. Titles may be bound into volumes and shelved in a special section, or on the regular shelves according to their classification number. To save space, many libraries prefer to subscribe to a microform edition that they keep in a permanent file, allowing the regular edition to be circulated and eventually discarded.

MAPS

Maps come in many forms: small sheets, large sheets, folders, wall maps, and globes. Many libraries do not catalog maps, but add them to a file arranged by geographical area. Larger or more important maps may be cataloged according to normal rules using the Chief Source of Information (Figure 4-2). The scale of a map should be recorded in the MATHEMATICAL DATA AREA, located immediately after the edition area. Use this area only in cartographic materials, and if the scale is not easily determined, omit this detail. Precede with the word "scale": Scale: 1 inch to the mile or 1:160,000. When several maps are cataloged as a unit simply indicate: Scales vary.

CONTROLLING NONBOOK MATERIALS

Faced with a variety of nonstandard packaging, unfamiliar labeling, and unavailable copy, many librarians leave nonbook materials uncataloged, shelved in a way appropriate to local practice, and available to selected users only. It is better to create a standard record, at Level One if necessary, than leave materials uncataloged. Following AACR2, a standard record can be created that will be adequate for networking purposes. This record can later be enhanced to a full record if necessary.

The following examples are standard records, providing enough bibliographic details for the average user.

```
    The Fabulous 60's [videorecording]  /  MPI Home Video.
      -- Maljack Productions.  [198-?].
      10 cassettes (60 min. each)  :  sd.,  col. ;  $\frac{1}{2}$ in.

      Documents events in the U.S. during the 1960's.
    One videocassette represents one year.
```

This item is cataloged at Level One, except for the physical description area, where each piece of information was judged important to the user. No date appeared in the material and the cataloger indicated the probable decade.

143

```
Art in action [picture].  -- Coronado Pub., 1987.
   30 art reproductions  :  col.  ; 61 x 46 cm.
+ teacher's manual.

   Enrichment Program II.
   30 art reproductions with background information
about each for classroom use.
```

Level One with enhanced physical description.

```
Rose, Gerald.
   The tiger skin rug  [filmstrip].  -- Encyclopedia
Britannica Educational Corp., 1980.
   1 filmstrip  :  col.  +  sound cassette (6:25 min.).

   A tiger leaves his home in the jungle and joins
a human family posing as their tiger skin rug.
```

Cataloged from title frame and cassette label.

```
The Weavers.
   Goodnight Irene [sound recording]. -- MCA, 1983.
   1 cassette.

   Contents: Tyena, Tyena, Tyena -- Goodnight
Irene -- The frozen logger -- Wreck of the John B.
-- Midnight special -- Follow the drinking gourd.
```

Level One allows notes as complete as the cataloger wishes. The main entry illustrates a corporate entry.

KITS

KITS contain two or more categories of materials packaged as a unit with a unit title. Normally the components are intended to be used together and no format is considered predominant. When this is the case, use the container title as the collective title for the item. List the formats making up the kit in the physical description area, adding no further description.

```
World War I, the home front [kit]. -- Social
   Issues Resource Series, [198-].
   5 posters, 1 sketch, 6 photographs, 1 newsheet,
19 documents, 2 sound cassettes + teacher's guide,
in container.

   24 exercises based on reproductions of
documents from the National Archives of years 1919
to 1929. Intended for secondary school students.
```

If a complete physical description of every item is necessary, give each a separate line.

Sometimes, however, cataloging entire kits leads to trouble at the circulation desk. Perhaps the user wants only part of a kit, or the size makes it difficult to manage. Kits and similar items may be separated and the sections processed, cataloged, and circulated separately. For example, a school owns a cassette filmstrip series on the five Scandinavian countries entitled *Northwest Europe*. This set can logically be broken into five items, with the cataloger supplying the titles Norway, Sweden, etc. Formats can also be cataloged separately. If a set arrives with study posters, these can be separated and cataloged using the GMD [picture].

RE-CATALOGING AND RE-CLASSIFYING MATERIALS

Decisions involved in re-cataloging and re-classifying have been discussed elsewhere. Whatever the philosophical approach to this problem, a certain amount will always be necessary, and this requires a careful change of each record. Besides changes made on the item itself, the shelf list record, each catalog entry, and any other record that has this information must be changed. If this is not done accurately and completely there will be such confusion about the item that it would have been better to have made no change at all. Large libraries have defined programs for reclassification and often have paraprofessional staff to assist. In a small institution, this is another task to be fitted into the daily workload. No matter what the situation, there should be a written procedure to prevent mishap. The same procedures are followed when an item is withdrawn; this time, however, the record is not changed, but removed. Some librarians leave records in the catalog long after an item has disappeared, in the expectation it will someday return. This is really not fair to the user, who may spend a great deal of time searching for a work that is no longer available. When an item is withdrawn, record this on the shelf list card so that if the item reappears bibliographic information is still available.

145

TYPING CARDS

Even those libraries that rely on purchased copy or central processing services find that they acquire some materials for which catalog cards must be typed. These typewritten cards should be made to the same specifications as the printed ones.

When possible, catalog at Level One. There are three INDENTIONS on a typed card. Normally the first indention is nine spaces from the left edge, the second indention is twelve spaces, and the third indention is fourteen spaces (see Figure 11-1).

Skeleton Card Showing Indentions

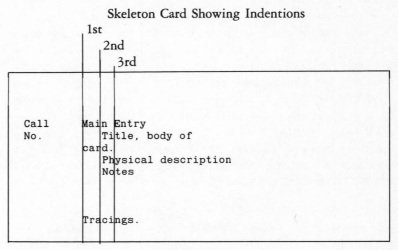

Figure 11-1

The call number is typed two spaces in from the left edge of the card on the third line down from the top. The main entry begins on the third line from the top of the card at first indention. If the main entry is longer than one line, the second line begins at third indention.

When main entry is under personal name or corporate body, the title is typed on the line below at second indention. The body of the card follows after the title, with the next lines brought back to the first indention, making a paragraph form. Remember each element is separated by a full stop (. −−).

Physical description follows the body of the card and begins at second indention. Depending on space, notes usually follow one full line below, beginning at the second indention. If longer than one full line, continue at first indention.

When main entry is under title, all other lines begin at second indention. This spacing, discussed in Chapter 2, is known as hanging indention.

Tracings are typed at least three lines below the catalog information at first indention. When there is no room on the face of the card, tracings may be typed on the back. Subject headings and added entries above the main entry begin at second indention. If they are too long for one line, continue on the second line at third indention.

Each library draws up its own typing manual, and there are probably no two libraries that follow exactly the same rules. Unless starting a new collection, study established cataloging rules. Unfortunately, in some libraries, no rules seem to have been established at all. In such a case, follow the guidelines above, and produce typed cards as uniformly and as neatly as possible.

PREPARING ANALYTICS

Users of large, diverse library collections seldom go away empty-handed. A small collection serves many demands, but has fewer items to meet these needs, so it is essential to extend the catalog information available to users.

There are reference works such as *Essay and General Literature Index*, *Biography Index*, and short story, play, and poetry indexes that can serve as supplements to the catalog. Shelve these nearby and indicate which collections are owned by the library in the list of those books indexed. These not only guide users to parts of books not analyzed in the catalog, but can also serve as a buying guide for the librarian.

Sometimes, in an effort to serve more users with fewer materials, and to avoid answering numerous questions about the location of a popular short story, catalogers make ANALYTIC ENTRIES, that is, entries in the catalog that provide access points to parts of collective works. Analytics are most often prepared for anthologies. Analytic cards cannot be purchased and must be prepared in individual libraries according to their needs. The following are examples of their use.

Subject Analytics

There are books, films, and filmstrips concerned with caring for every conceivable kind of pet, and some libraries may own a variety of these. Others may own only a few general items about pets. In order that these general materials can serve those users searching for only "hamsters" or "mice" in addition to the subject heading "pets," analytic subject entries are made for the individual pets included.

Collective biographies are usually given a general heading, such as ARTISTS, FRENCH. In a small collection, a subject analytic entry can be made for each individual artist discussed.

147

Author / Title :
Title / Author
Analytics

Students may be assigned individual plays to read and come to the library to look for them. The library may purchase plays only in collections, as the cost per play is less. Since the students may look under either the author or the title of the desired play, entries are made under author/title, and in reverse under the title/author. These are typed as headings, above the main entry, e.g.,

*Author and
title analytic:*

Sherwood, Robert
    The petrified forest

*Title and author
analytic:*

    The petrified forest
Sherwood, Robert

Title Analytics

For a collection of works by one author, title analytics can be made for each individual work. The author's name is the main entry.

Romeo and Juliet
Shakespeare, William
    Shakespeare's tragedies

Typing Analytics
and Cross
References

Ideally, analytics are simply added to a unit card by typing the additional information above the main entry at second indention. Two-line author and title analytics are typed two lines above the main entry at the second and third indention. Title and author entries are made at third and second. If all of the card must be typed, use a truncated form, giving only call number, main entry, title, publisher, and date.

When cross reference cards are used in the catalog to refer users either from terms and names not used (*see* references), or to related terms that might be useful (*see also*), they must also be typed. Type the term not used three lines from the top of the card at the second indention. Two lines below, and at the third indention, type *see*. Two lines below this, and at the first indention, type the term used.

Oxford book of American verse
    see

The New Oxford book of American verse

Follow exactly the same format for *see also* references. Type all subjects in capital letters.

```
        FAMILY
            see also
        CLANS AND CLAN SYSTEM
        HOME
        PARENT AND·CHILD
```

```
        FAMILY

            see also

        names of members of the family, e.g.,
        CHILDREN, FATHERS, etc.
```

Creasey wrote under many names, and some libraries will pull these forms together for the user. *See also* cards can either be filed following, or in front of, entries of the same word, phrase, or name.

```
        Creasey, John

            see also

        Ashe, Gordon·
        Halliday, Michael
        Hunt, Kyle
        Marric, J. J.
        Morton, Anthony
        York, Jeremy
```

Since most automated systems do not allow for the creation of analytics, these records have largely disappeared with the advent of electronic catalogs. Unfortunately, the need for them has not. Librarians need to acquire the various indexes to collections that are available and make their users aware of their contents. Often a small manual file of analytics maintained at the reference or circulation desk can save hours of time in searching.

FILING

Whether entries are duplicates, original cataloging, or analytics, they must be filed in the catalog to be useful. The tool for filing is the latest edition of *ALA Filing Rules*. Filing can be confusing in a large dictionary catalog. The confusion is lessened when the catalog is divided into one selection for author/title, and another for subject, because subject entries are usually not filed in strict alphabetical order, but according to special rules.

All catalogs are filed either WORD BY WORD or LETTER BY LETTER. Most users are unaware of the distinction, yet it can make a considerable difference to the order in which entries are found.

149

Word by Word	*Letter by Letter*
San Diego	Sanchez, George Isadore
San Domingo	Sand, George
San Francisco	Sandburg, Carl
Sanchez, George Isadore	Sande, Earl
Sand, George	San Diego
Sandburg, Carl	San Domingo
Sande, Earl	San Francisco

When filing word by word, the rule is "nothing before something." With word-by-word filing, San Francisco is filed before Sanchez because of the space (nothing) after San. Letter-by-letter filing ignores spaces. Most card catalogs are filed word by word, whereas many reference sources file letter by letter. The basic principle of the rules is to "file as is," although previous filing practice stressed filing "as if." For example, formerly Dr. was filed as if it were written Doctor, Mr. as if it were Mister, and the numeral 4 as if it were written four. In the 1980 rules numerals are filed before letters, roman numerals are treated as if they were arabic, and written numbers are filed alphabetically. Words that can be spelled in different ways (i.e., honour or honor), and abbreviations, are filed exactly as written. The rules recommend liberal use of information cards and *see* and *see also* references to guide users.

Filing "as is" will in the long run make a difficult task simpler for both filer and user. However, it will not solve every filing problem. Considering that an entry misfiled is an item lost, it is good practice to study the structure of any catalog before attempting to file, and to have a copy of the rules to help with such problems as filing Teofile de la Toore, José de la Torre Bueno, and DeKalb, Illinois. For accuracy, file twice, once above the rod, and make a second check before dropping the cards.

SUMMARY

Original cataloging, adapting copy, preparing reports, and keeping records require professional training or attention, but there are other tasks of stamping, bar-coding, typing, and pasting that must be accomplished if the library is to function smoothly. Even libraries that rely on a central agency for processing and record-keeping find many procedures must still be done at the local level, and require efficient organization and planning to be fitted into the work schedule.

Circulation records are created to inform librarians what has been lent to users. They also generate more files to be maintained. Serials are usually locally received, and can be expensive if inaccurately checked-in and controlled. Unless there is a good reason to spend time and money on inventory-taking, it should not be done routinely.

No matter how catalog copy is acquired, the individual library is responsible for analytics and *see* and *see also* references. These should not be done routinely, but only to give service and save time.

Cataloging serials, kits, and maps requires special attention, since serial entries must reflect holdings, maps need scale location, and kits are often more useful if broken into components.

Those who must still file cards should understand the structure of the catalog and follow the 1980 ALA guidelines, which simplify the rules and make more sense to patrons.

Computers can generate many statistics. Librarians need to analyze and justify those that help them to improve practice.

CHAPTER REVIEW

Terms to understand:

alphabetic designation	letter by letter
analytics	mathematical data area
chronological designation	numeric designation
claiming	open entry
duplicates	periodicals
indention	serials
item record	visible file
kit	word by word

The shelf list record:

Records each item, whether a duplicate title or not.
Provides an inventory of the collection.
Must be kept current.

Circulation records:

Record materials that are lent to users.
Are designed according to a library's need for information: for example, some libraries are interested only in overdue circulation records.

Serials records:

Must be kept current. Users must know titles and dates in collections. Librarians must make sure issues arrive.

Inventory records and statistics:

Should be kept only when they supply useful information for decision making, or when required by law.

Analytics:

When practical, provide access to parts of the content of materials, either by author of a part, subject of a part, or title of a part.

Filing:

File according to the latest *ALA Filing Rules*. Be consistent: file either word by word or letter by letter. File *as is*, not *as if*.

CHAPTER 12

CATALOGING NEW TECHNOLOGIES

IN THIS time of rapid change, new technologies constantly arrive to be added to the library's collection. Rules will not always be available and prepared cataloging copy may never appear. It has taken several years to agree on terminology and format for cataloging computer software programs, and it will take time to agree on rules for other emerging technologies.

In the initial AACR2, Chapter 9, "Machine-Readable Data Files," was outdated on publication. The spectacular growth of personal computer ownership and accompanying disc software superseded mainframes very quickly and catalogers were struggling to organize this new format under inadequate rules. Composed for mainframes, with storage consisting of magnetic tape or punched cards, the 1978 rules meant little to those dealing with Pacman or Logo; and the GMD "machine-readable data file" (MRDF) had little significance to users searching for software programs. The crisis was so evident that a separate Chapter 9 was published as soon as the committees could agree on rules for the new technology. The revised AACR2 (1988) refers to COMPUTER FILES and provides guidelines for the familiar sorts of computer programs available in many library collections. In AACR2 a computer file is defined as a data or program file encoded for manipulation by computers, and the general material designator has been changed to the simple "computer file." It still remains for the cataloger to make clear to users what hardware the programs require, and this is accomplished in the physical description area and the notes. Generally it is necessary to catalog those software items that circulate to the library's users, but it is not essential to catalog library management programs not available to them.

CATALOGING COMPUTER FILES

The following suggestions are offered for those wishing to integrate commercially produced software programs into an omni catalog, following standard rules, without excessive detail, but with sufficient information for the average user.

The title screen is the preferred Chief Source of Information. In reality, however, many catalogers must operate without access to computer equipment, and many title screens scroll by so rapidly that bibliographic details are difficult to obtain. Either the physical carrier itself or its labels are the second choice, with the publisher's or creator's documentation the third choice for sources of information. Should these sources not agree, choose the one that contains the most information.

Here is an example of a computer program called Logo showing the information available from the title screen (Figure 12-1) and the documentation title page (Figure 12-2).

Title Screen

```
IBM Personal Computer Logo Version 1.00
© Copyright IBM Corp. 1983
© Copyright LCSI 1983
Serial Number 0767380521


WELCOME TO LOGO
?****************************************
****************************************
****************************************
************
```

Figure 12-1

Software Documentation Title Page

IBM   *Personal Computer*
                                         Education Series

Logo

by Logo Computer Systems, Inc.

Figure 12-2

```
005.133 LOGO [computer file] / LOGO Systems.
LOG         -- Version 1.00. -- IBM, 1983.
            1 disk + 1 loose leaf binder. -- (Personal
       computer education series)

            IBM personal computer LOGO reference.
            Systems requirements: 128K ; DOS 2.00 ;
       color monitor.

            1. LOGO (Computer program language)
       I. Title  II. IBM PC.
```

Figure 12-3

Logo is cataloged in Figure 12-3 at Level One, always recommended when appropriate for those doing original cataloging. In this case, the title screen (Figure 12-1) and the title page of the documentation (Figure 12-2) provide the bibliographic details: the title, "LOGO"; the statement of responsibility, "by Logo Computer Systems, Inc."; and series "Personal Computer Education Series" are from the title page. The title screen also provides the edition information "IBM Personal Computer Logo version 1.00" and the first copyright statement, which furnishes information for the publication, distribution, etc. area.

Physical Description

Preparing a physical description for a new format can often pose problems for a cataloger. Informing users of the number of pages, the presence of illustrations, and the size of a book have long been agreed upon, but it is less clear what physical details a patron will expect a catalog to provide about other information formats. First Level of description requires only that the extent of the item be recorded. When dealing with computer files, simply record the number of units followed by an appropriate descriptive term such as computer disk, computer reel, or computer cassette. More details can be added such as sound (sd.), color (col.), or dimensions, but these are optional. Always list accompanying materials, either here or in the notes. Both patrons and librarians need to be aware of the number and types of items involved. Most library users will be satisfied to know what kind of item it is and what equipment is needed to play it.

The subject heading is taken from directions provided in the 13th edition of *Sears* and the call number from a revision of the 20th edition of Dewey that provides numbers for specific programming languages. A title card is necessary only if the library has a divided catalog and the added entry for IBM PC answers the question, "What do you have that runs on my IBM PC?"

Cataloged at Level One using the container, the example in Figure 12-4 uses *Sears* subject headings and the abridged DDC. The

```
567.9   Dinosaur dig [computer file]. -- CBS
DIN        Software, 1984.
           2 computer disks + 1 plastic keyboard overlay
        + 1 program guide + 1 teacher's guide + 2 backup
        disks.
        ISBN 0-03-007657-9

           System requirements: Apple II+; IIe; 48K;
        diskdrive; monitor.

        1. Dinosaurs--Computer assisted instruction
        I. Apple II+  II. Apple IIe.
```

Figure 12-4

standard number is usually listed when found. A divided catalog would need an extra card added in the tracing for the title. It's not necessary to seek out alternative subject heading lists or classification numbers when cataloging computer files or other electronic software. Simply assign the appropriate Dewey number or subject heading according to the content.

Computer software is one of those areas for which the material (or type of publication) specific details area may be used to indicate the type of file. When available, one of the following terms can be recorded: computer file, computer program(s), or computer date and program(s). If a GMD has been used, the word computer may be dropped, but only if the information is readily available given the number or approximate number of files that make up the content.

computer data (1 file: 500 records)
computer program (2 files: 600 statements)

Each month advertisements in library literature describe new information formats to replace or join the more familiar ones. Librarians are constantly making preparations to introduce yet another type of technology to their users. Sooner or later, after problems of equipment and cost have been faced, come the problems of integrating the format into the existing catalog. There is usually a delay between the introduction of a new format into the collection and the development of rules for cataloging it.

Chapter 1 of AACR2 provides the best approach to solving this problem. Follow the basic steps of examining the item, and search for the bibliographic details that are closest to the item itself: a title screen, a label attached by the producer, a title frame, and so forth. Second in order of preference is the container, and third is the documentation accompanying the item. Cataloging at Level One is best, because it provides a standard description that can be amplified later if necessary. Although new technologies are unlikely

155

to have standard numbers assigned, collect any that are available and place them in the appropriate spot in the record. It is more difficult to decide on terminology for the physical description area and general material designator. In the case of a compact disc recording, the GMD most appropriate is [sound recording]; while a CD-ROM (compact disc–read only memory) information package would have the GMD [computer file]. In the case of new formats, rather than make up terminology for the specific materials designation, check standard reference sources and indexes for the terms most widely used. LCSH introduces the subject heading CD-ROM in the 11th edition, so that term then can be used for the specific material designator in the physical description areas. Both *Sears* and LCSH use the term compact disc for recordings and that term as well as an indication of the size of the disc will alert users to the technology of the item being described. Other places to check for terminology standards are the *Readers' Guide to Periodical Literature* and standard periodical indexes. Periodicals publish the most recent information about new technologies, and standard subject headings are quickly added to the indexes. At Level One minimal physical description is necessary, but there must be enough information to be useful to the users. For example, in the new technologies, equipment is often not standard and exact specifications are necessary.

Patrons not only want to check out computer files, but they also want to read about them. In response to the great increase in publications in the field of computer science, *Dewey Decimal Classification* found it necessary to develop a new schedule, moving computer science from 001.6 to 004 and expanding it from two pages to fourteen. Issued separately as a revision of the 19th edition, the new schedule is included in the 20th edition.

Searching
Computer Catalogs

In addition to cataloging electronic formats, libraries also store their records in an electronic catalog. In the rush to automate, the needs of the user may be overlooked. Patrons accustomed to sorting through catalogs by the standard access points of author, title, and subject may be confused when presented with a catalog that instead calls for "query formation for relevant retrieval strategies relying on Boolean operators." One problem is that vendors have made available a great variety of electronic catalogs, each approached with different searching techniques.

An electronic database can be searched in one of three ways, MENU, COMMAND, or FREE TEXT. Most familiar is the menu approach, in which a user may choose among a number of options that appear on the screen. The "user friendly" menu approach requires a great deal of storage space, and is too slow to work well with a large amount of data. Free text searching can also be user friendly because the user need only type in a word and records will appear. But in a large database, unless some sort of search strategy is designed, a large number of irrelevant records may appear.

Most electronic catalogs provide for free text searching but rely basically on the command approach for which the computer has been programmed to respond to certain commands typed in by the user. Unfortunately there is no standard for commands, and these vary widely from system to system. For example, commands for an author search can vary in many ways, such as:

Find Author
F A
Au =
S A
Search Au

The computer will respond only to the exact command. Commands can become quite complex, and the user must first be told what they are, perhaps by a help screen, manual, or chart. Unlike searching the card catalog, electronic catalogs offer users a variety of approaches, and patrons that use a number of library systems may find they need to learn different commands for each. This has implications for staffing, for design of the system, and for programs of library instruction.

SUMMARY

Automation and the development of bibliographic utilities have solved many cataloging problems. Libraries can now purchase standard cataloging copy, conforming to current practice, for library materials in many formats. This is of little comfort, however, to those who must organize collections of materials produced in-house, who catalog in libraries that acquire new formats more rapidly than rules can be devised to describe them, or who work in libraries with few cataloging resources or no access to automation. Five common-sense rules apply in these situations:

1. *When possible, create a standard minimal level (Level One) of description.*
Level One records are standard records, with standard access points that can be filed or entered in any catalog. They answer the basic questions of most library users, "Who created this item, what is the title, edition, and year of publication, and in what format is it?" and, since they demand less bibliographic details, they are simpler and faster to produce. Any additional information required, such as grade level or contents, can be added in the notes area. At a later

date, if more details are needed, or if new rules appear, these records can normally be enhanced rather than redone.

2. *Standardize main and added entries according to* AACR2.
Library users assume the catalog can tell them how many items by a certain author, or how many editions of an individual title, are in the library. This is only true if headings have been standardized. Records created according to AACR2 will be standard in the majority of libraries, rarely need to be redone later, and can be shared among institutions. They meet the needs of users, who will also be provided with some consistency between library catalogs.

3. *Use a standard authority file for subject headings.*
Subject access is more difficult to provide for library items than author or title access. Virtually all librarians simplify the task by using some sort of standard list. The most common are *Sears* and the Library of Congress. LC subject headings are also readily available in CIP copy, on purchased cards, and in the bibliographic databases.

4. *Record on the shelf list card any standard number found on the item.*
No matter what the present situation, automation is in the future for most libraries. Each year the sale of printed cards decreases and the demand for machine-readable records grows. Standard machine-readable records are most easily and economically retrieved from the databases by using standard numbers such as the ISBN, the LC card number, or the Superintendent of Documents number. Recording these on the shelf list now will facilitate automation in the future.

5. *Match available cataloging copy to item in hand.*
While it is tempting for the busy librarian to use cataloging copy as is, this can defeat the purpose of providing a catalog at all. Editions and physical description may differ, titles may reflect an earlier series, authors' names may be recorded according to older rules.

If such differences are not corrected when the records are placed in the catalog, a number of problems will arise later. Inventory may prove confusing and inaccurate, users may spend time searching for an item the library doesn't really have, and it will be almost impossible to gather items together bibliographically in the catalog. Automation is difficult and expensive when records do not match items.

The future will bring still more changes in the form of library catalogs, as well as in formats of the materials they describe. However, descriptions of library materials will remain standard, answering the basic questions users have always had when trying to locate information in their library. The library that has created standard bibliographic records will be able to transfer and use these records into the next century, as catalog forms come and go.

CHAPTER REVIEW

Terms to understand:

command	free text
computer files	menu

Cataloging computer files:

Catalog at Level One, record other necessary information in the notes, and record standard numbers.

Select bibliographic details from those closest to the item itself.

Cataloging new formats:

Catalog at Level One, following Chapter 1 in AACR2, and select terminology from current indexes.

When faced with the chore of typing a set of catalog cards it is little comfort to know these occasions have become less frequent during the past decade. Directions for spacing and punctuation have been given elsewhere in this book; this section summarizes typing procedures.

Spacing between lines
Lines should be separated by single spacing, but if space permits leave two lines between the physical description and the notes, and at least three lines between end of catalog information and tracings.

Accent marks
If the typewriter has accent marks, type as written; otherwise add in ink.

Capitalization
In general, follow common usage, i.e., capitalize proper names and words derived from proper names, titles of people, historic events, first word of a sentence, or the beginning of a title of a work. Do not capitalize parts of titles that are not proper nouns.
In a title main entry, if the title begins with an article, the following word is also capitalized.

Abbreviations
Abbreviate standard terms as listed in section "Abbreviations."
Abbreviate names of states following names of places.
Abbreviate names of countries following foreign places.

Call numbers
Type the classification number on the third line from the top of the card, two spaces from the left-hand edge.
Type Cutter number, or book number, directly below the classification number.
Type any additional parts, such as date or volume number, directly below book numbers.
Use no punctuation except for the decimal in the class number, or a period after "v." (volume).

Series
Begin series area (in parentheses) after a full stop following physical description area.
Use no capitalization except for first word of series and for proper names.
If the series area runs over the line, return to first indention on next line.

Notes

Usually, notes begin two lines below the physical description, starting at the second indention.

Given in paragraph form, each note beginning a new line at second indention and continuing at first indention if it runs over.

In content notes, standard ISBD punctuation is followed.

Tracings

Arrange in paragraph form.

Type these at least three lines below the catalog information at first indention.

If there is no room on the face of the card, type them on the back of the card near the bottom, so the card can be tilted forward and the tracings easily read.

Tracings are numbered: arabic numbers for subjects, roman numerals for added entries.

Tracings should be typed on the main entry card and on the shelf list card.

Added cards

If there is too much information to go on one catalog card, it is continued on a second card. Type at the point of break: "Continued on next card."

On the second card type the call number, the main entry, title and date. In parentheses, add "Card 2" two spaces below contents.

Use of stamps

Never type when a stamp will do. Frequently used information, such as "Ask at desk," or "Reference," can be stamped either above the call number or as a note.

Completing Prepared Printed Cards

1. The Main Entry Card.
   Leave one card as is except for typing in the call number.
   This is the main entry card.
2. Subject Cards.
   When making a subject card, type the subject heading one line above the main entry at second indention.
   Type subject headings in capital letters, spelling all words in full, including those abbreviated in the tracing.
   If the subject will occupy more than one line, begin at the second line above the main entry, and begin the run-on line directly below at the third indention.
3. Name-Added Entries.
   If, after a name, there is a designation "joint author," it follows after the name of the person in the added entry card.

4. Title Entries.
   The word "title" in the tracings indicates that a title card is an added entry. On the line above the main entry, beginning at second indention, type the title. If it runs onto the second line, start two lines above the main entry and continue on the next line at third indention.
5. Series.
   If there is an entry made for a series, only the word "series" is found in the tracings. In that case, type the series title above the main entry matching the series title as given in the series area on the card.

When all the cards must be typed, prepare only the shelf list and main entry card in full. On all other added entry cards, stop after recording the date. This produces a truncated record. Users can see the whole record on the main entry card.

Typing
a Complete Set
of Cards

General abbreviations that are standard usage in cataloging:

abridged	abr.
approximately	approx.
black and white	b&w
book	bk.
centimeters	cm.
chapter	ch.
colored, coloured	col.
company	co.
compiler	comp.
copyright	c
corporation	corp.
edition	ed.
enlarged	enl.
frame	fr.
illustration(s)	ill.
introduction	introd.
Limited	Ltd.
no name (of publisher)	s.n.
no place (of publication)	s.l.
photographs	photos.
preface	pref.
revised	rev.
series	ser.
silent	si.
sound	sd.
supplement	suppl.
volume(s)	v.

ALA Filing Rules. Filing Committee Resources and Technical Services Division. American Library Association. Chicago, American Library Association, 1980.

Anglo-American Cataloguing Rules. 2nd rev. ed. Edited by Michael Gorman and Paul Winkler. Chicago, American Library Association, 1988.

Arksley, Laura. "The Library of Assurbanipal." *Wilson Library Bulletin* 51 (June 1977), pp. 833–840.

Austin, Derek and Jeremy A. Digger. "PRECIS: The Preserved Context Index System." *Library Resources and Technical Services* 21 (Winter 1977), pp. 13–30.

Barden, Bertha R. *Book Numbers: A Manual for Students with a Basic Code of Rules.* Chicago, American Library Association, 1932.

Bloomberg, Marty. *Introduction to Technical Services for Library Technicians.* 5th ed. Littleton, Colo., Libraries Unlimited, Inc., 1985.

Bloomberg, Marty and Hans Weber. *An Introduction to Classification and Number Building in Dewey.* Littleton, Colo., Libraries Unlimited, Inc., 1976.

Crawford, Walt. *MARC for Library Use: Understanding the USMARC Format.* White Plains, NY, Knowledge Industries, 1984.

Curley, Arthur and Jean Varlejs. *Aker's Simple Library Cataloging.* 7th ed. Scarecrow, Metuchen, N. J., 1985.

Cutter, Charles A. *Alphabetic Order Table Altered and Fitted with Three Figures by Kate Sanborn.* (Obtained from H. R. Huntting Co., Chicopee Falls, Mass.)

Dewey, Melvil. *Dewey Decimal Classification and Relative Index.* 11th abridged ed. Forest Press, Inc., a division of OCLC, Online Computer Library Center, 1979.

Dewey, Melvil. *Dewey Decimal Classification and Relative Index.* 20th ed. Forest Press, Inc., a division of OCLC, Online Computer Library Center, 1989.

Dowell, Arlene G. and Rosanna M. Oneil. *Cataloging with Copy, a Decision-Maker's Handbook.* 2nd ed. Littleton, Colo., Libraries Unlimited, Inc., 1988.

Dunkin, Paul S. *Cataloging U.S.A.* Chicago, American Library Association, 1969.

Fayen, Emily Gallup. *The Online Catalog: Improving Public Access to*

Library Materials. White Plains, N.Y., Knowledge Industries, 1983.

Hunter, Eric J. *Computer Cataloging*. London, Clive Bingley, 1985.

Library of Congress. *Classification Class A–Z*. Washington, Government Printing Office, 1904 to date.

Library of Congress. *Subject Cataloging Manual* (rev. ed.). Washington, Subject Cataloging Division, Processing Department, Library of Congress.

Library of Congress. *Subject Headings Used in the Dictionary Catalogs of the Library of Congress*. Washington, Subject Cataloging Division, Processing Department, Library of Congress.

Marshall, Joan. *On Equal Terms: A Thesaurus for Non-Sexist Indexing and Cataloging*. New York, Neal-Schuman, 1977.

Matthews, Joseph R. *Choosing an Automated Library System: A Planning Guide*. Chicago, American Library Association, 1980.

Miller, Edward. *Prince of Librarians: The Life and Times of Antonio Panizzi of the British Museum*. Athens, Ohio, Ohio University Press, 1974.

Norris, Dorothy May. *A History of Cataloguing and Cataloguing Methods 1100–1880: With an Introductory Survey of Ancient Times*. London, Grafton, 1936.

Oddy, R. N. et al. *Information Retrieval Research*. London, Butterworth, 1981.

Olson, Nancy B. *Cataloging of Audiovisual Materials Supplement Coding and Tagging for OCLC*, Mankato, Minn., Minnesota Scholarly Press, 1985.

Olson, Nancy B. et al. *Cataloging of Audiovisual Materials; a Manual Based on AARC2*. 2nd ed. rev. and expanded. Mankato, Minn., Minnesota Scholarly Press, 1985.

Piercy, Esther J. *Commonsense Cataloging*. 2nd ed. rev. by Marion Sanner. New York, H. W. Wilson, 1974.

RTSD/CCS Cataloging of Children's Materials Committee. "Guidelines for Standardized Cataloging of Children's Materials." *Top of the News* 40 no. 1 (Fall 1983).

Sears List of Subject Headings. 13th ed. Edited by Carmen Rovira and Caroline Reyes. New York, H. W. Wilson, 1986.

Young, Micki Jo. *Introduction to Microcomputers in Federal Libraries*. Washington, Library of Congress, 1978.

American Book Publishing Record (BPR). New York, R. R. Bowker Company, 1960 to date.

Book Review Digest. New York, H. W. Wilson Company, 1905 to date.

The Booklist. Chicago, American Library Association, 1905 to date.

Children's Catalog. 15th ed. New York, H. W. Wilson Company, 1986.

Fiction Catalog. 11th ed. New York, H. W. Wilson Company, 1986.

Junior High School Library Catalog. 5th ed. New York, H. W. Wilson Company, 1985.

Public Library Catalog. 8th ed. New York, H. W. Wilson Company, 1984.

Senior High School Library Catalog. 13th ed. New York, H. W. Wilson Company, 1987.

Weekly Record. New York, R. R. Bowker Company, 1974 to date. Weekly.

ACCESS POINT—A term under which a bibliographic record is filed.

ACCESSION NUMBER—A number assigned to each item in a collection in order of its receipt in the library.

ACCOMPANYING MATERIALS—Any materials, such as answer sheets, pictures, or instructions, issued with and intended to be used with an item to be cataloged.

ADDED ENTRY—A catalog entry other than the main or subject entry; includes titles, joint authors, series, etc.

ALTERNATIVE TITLE—A second title introduced by "or" or its equivalent.

ANALYTIC ENTRY—A catalog entry for a part of a work, entered under the author, title, or subject of the part.

ANGLO-AMERICAN CATALOGUING RULES, 2nd rev. ed. (AACR2)—The official American cataloging code, covering both description and access points for eleven formats of materials.

ANNOTATED CARD PROGRAM (AC)—A service of the Library of Congress that provides subject headings tailored for juvenile material.

AREA TABLE—Table II notations from the DDC applied to other notations to designate geographical areas.

AUTHOR ENTRY—The name of the author of a work used as the filing name in the catalog; often the main entry.

AUTHOR SERIES—A series of books written by one author and issued under a collective title, e.g., The Story of Civilization.

AUTHORITY FILE—A record of names or terms used as catalog entries; maintained in order to ensure uniformity.

AUXILIARY TABLES—Tables that present possible sub-arrangements within subjects, used in classification.

BASE NUMBER—From the DDC. That portion of a number in a sequence which does not vary as other digits are added as instructed.

BIBLIOGRAPHIC DETAILS—Those features of a work such as title, author, edition, publisher, date, and series used for identification and description.

BIBLIOGRAPHIC UTILITY—A service organization that maintains large online files of bibliographic data.

BOOK CATALOG—A library catalog in the form of a book.

BOOK NUMBER—Part of a call number used to arrange materials with the same classification number in alphabetical order.

CALL NUMBER—The number (composed of letters, numbers, or symbols) used to identify and locate a library item.

CARD CATALOG—A library catalog of cards. An entry, or record, is placed on each card.

CATALOGING IN PUBLICATION (CIP)—Cataloging data on the verso of the title page, furnished by the Library of Congress.

CATALOGING PROFILE—Cataloging and/or processing specifications developed for an individual library.

CD-ROM (Compact Disc—Read Only Memory)—An optically based electronic medium, with massive storage capacity, that can be locally accessed with a computer attached to a compact disc player, thus avoiding the communication costs of using a remote online system. Some library catalogs are contained on CD-ROMs.

CHIEF SOURCE OF INFORMATION—The place prescribed by AACR2 to look for information to use when cataloging an item, such as the title page of a book or the label on a film can.

CHRONOLOGICAL DESIGNATION—An area of descriptive cataloging for serials that identifies the item by date or number (or both) of issue.

CLAIMING—The process of notifying a jobber, subscription service, or publisher that serial issues are missing.

CLASSED CATALOG—A catalog arranged by subject or classification number.

CLASSIFICATION—The grouping of materials by subject or form, usually according to DDC or LCC.

CLOSED SHELVES—Areas housing library materials that are not accessible to the public.

COLLECTION—A distinct group of books or other materials; may also refer to a library's entire holdings.

COLLECTIVE TITLE—An inclusive title under which several works, each of which may have an individual title, are published.

COLLECTIVE WORK—An item that contains either three or more independent parts by one author or two or more independent parts by more than one author.

COM CAT—Computer output microform catalog. A catalog produced by a computer either on fiche or microfilm.

COMMAND—A word or symbol for which a computer has been programmed to respond.

COMPACT DISC—*See* CD-ROM.

COMPUTER FILES—Data or program files encoded for manipulation by computers.

COMPUTER NETWORK—A complex consisting of two or more usually physically dispersed computer systems, terminals, and communication facilities linked by telecommunications channels to enable shared data processing and storage.

CORPORATE ENTRY—The name of a corporate body used as a catalog entry.

CROSS REFERENCES—Referrals from terms or names not used in a particular catalog or index to those that are. See *See* and *See also.*

CUTTER TABLE—A list of letters and numbers assigned to names of authors to form parts of call numbers.

DATABASE—A set of machine-readable records contained in a computer file directly searchable through a terminal.

DDC—The Dewey Decimal Classification system; a system of notation used to classify library materials.

DESCRIPTIVE CATALOGING—Providing a description and establishing access points for library materials.

DICTIONARY CATALOG—A catalog in which all entries, including author, title, and subject, are filed in a single alphabet.

DIVIDED CATALOG—A catalog divided into parts. Usually one part contains author, title, and other added entries, and a second part contains subject entries.

DUPLICATE—An item identical to another in content, format, etc. Often used to refer to additional copies of a work.

EASY BOOK—A book for young children, usually consisting primarily of pictures.

EDITION—The entire number of identical copies of a work produced in one or several printings.

ELEMENTS OF DESCRIPTION—The eight areas employed when describing an item in descriptive cataloging. These areas are: title and statement of responsibility; edition; material (or type of publication) specific details (applicable only to cartographic materials, serials, computer files, and printed music); publication, distribution, etc.; physical description; series; notes; and standard number and terms of availability.

ENTRY—A bibliographic record of an item in a catalog.

EXTENT OF THE ITEM—First element of the physical description area; gives number and specific material designation of the item being described.

FILING TITLE—A standard title assigned to a work that has appeared under various titles to identify it in the catalog.

FIXED FIELD—In an electronic database, a field that is restricted as to the number of characters. *See also* VARIABLE FIELD.

FIXED LOCATION—An arrangement of library materials in which each item is assigned a permanent location.

FREE TEXT SEARCHING—Searching a database using key words or terms rather than words or terms selected from a controlled list.

GENERAL MATERIAL DESIGNATIONS [GMD]—A term indicating a broad, general class of material to which an item belongs, e.g., text, microform, etc.

GENERAL REFERENCES—*See* and *see also* notations given in *Sears* that give blanket directions for all headings in a certain group that lead to other, related headings to be searched.

HANGING INDENTION—The form used for a catalog card on which the title is the main entry and is the only line of the description beginning at the first indention.

HEADING—Any word, name, or phrase placed at the head of a catalog entry to provide an access point.

INDENTION—The prescribed distance from the lefthand edge of a catalog card at which various cataloging elements should begin.

INPUT—Getting a program into the computer's memory, normally through a keyboard, a cassette tape recorder, or a disk drive.

INTERACTIVE CATALOG—Electronic catalog in which a user's commands elicit a response.

INTER-LIBRARY LOAN—Exchange of materials between libraries.

INTERNATIONAL STANDARD BIBLIOGRAPHIC DESCRIPTION (ISBD)—An international standard of punctuation for bibliographic records.

INTERNATIONAL STANDARD BOOK NUMBER (ISBN)—A code number uniquely assigned to a specific title or edition of a title.

INTERNATIONAL STANDARD SERIAL NUMBER (ISSN)—A code number uniquely assigned to a series.

ITEM RECORD—A record that identifies an individual item in the collection, usually employing some unique number designator.

KEYWORD SEARCH—A search for information retrieval, made possible by automation, in which individual words in any selected field of a bibliographic citation can serve as access points.

KIT—A multi-media item.

LCC—Library of Congress Cataloging.

LCSH—*Library of Congress Subject Headings*. Used in many college and university libraries.

LETTER-BY-LETTER FILING—An order of entries in which the space between words is ignored. The alternative to WORD-BY-WORD FILING.

LEVELS OF DESCRIPTION—Descriptive cataloging employs one of three levels of description, all of which use standard terminology. They range in completeness from First Level, which employs the minimum amount of information, to Third Level, the most detailed.

MACHINE-READABLE DATA—Data that can be directly interpreted by a computer system.

MAIN ENTRY—A complete catalog record of an item under the heading by which it will be uniformly identified.

MAIN FRAME—A large, powerful computer, capable of controlling other computer systems.

MARC (MAchine-Readable Cataloging)—A database of cataloging information distributed by the Library of Congress.

MATHEMATICAL DATA AREA—An area of descriptive cataloging, used only for cartographic material, in which scale and projection are recorded.

MENU—A list of options displayed by the computer to the user, who then selects the next operation.

MICROCOMPUTER—The smallest computer system, designed for a single user.

MICROFICHE—A microform issued as a card.

MICROFILM—A microform issued in a continuous strip.

MICROFORM CATALOG—A catalog produced in microform (either microfilm or microfiche) in a size too small to be read by the naked eye.

MIXED RESPONSIBILITY—Different persons contribute different kinds of activity to a work, i.e., writing and illustration.

MNEMONIC DEVICE—Anything that assists the memory.

MULTILEVEL DESCRIPTION—A method of noting accompanying materials in which there is complete identification, in one record, of all parts that share a common bibliographic entry.

NETWORKING—Linking libraries in order to share bibliographic data and materials.

NOTES—An area set up to record additional information, such as teacher's manuals, bibliographies, defective copy, etc.

NUMERIC AND/OR ALPHABETIC DESIGNATION—An area of descriptive cataloging that applies only to serials.

OCLC—Online Computer Library Center. A bibliographic network that shares cataloging among member libraries via online terminals.

OMNI CATALOG—A catalog in which records of all formats are found.

ONLINE COMPUTER CATALOG—Distribution of cataloging information by online computer transmission.

OPEN ENTRY—A catalog entry for a serial or set which has not yet completed publication; certain information will be filled in later.

OPEN SHELF—Library materials in areas open to the public.

ORIGINAL CATALOGING—The process of creating a catalog record without prepared copy supplied by a vendor.

OTHER PHYSICAL DETAILS—Provided when EXTENT OF THE ITEM is not enough. OTHER PHYSICAL DETAILS include length, sound, speed, etc.

OTHER TITLE INFORMATION—Any title on an item that is neither the title proper nor a parallel title.

OUTPUT—Supplying the results of the computer's work to the user.

PARALLEL TITLE—The title proper in another language or script.

PERIODICAL—A publication with a distinctive title intended to appear in successive numbers or parts at stated or regular intervals and for an indefinite time.

PHOENIX SCHEDULE—A completely new schedule in the DDC. Only the basic number for the discipline remains the same.

PHYSICAL DESCRIPTION—Identifying the physical characteristics of an item for cataloging purposes.

PRECIS—The Preserved Context Indexing System, a chain indexing system used to provide subject access to *The British National Bibliography*.

PRIME MARKS—Marks that indicate where DDC numbers (for instance, those included in the CIP data) can be shortened without losing the meaning (i.e., indication of sectional grouping of the item) of the notation.

PUBLISHER SERIES—A series of books by different authors issued under a collective title, e.g., Little Golden Books.

RECTO—Any righthand page in an open book. The reverse of VERSO.

RELATIVE INDEX—An index that reverses the subordination of subject to discipline by bringing together aspects of subjects from the disciplines used in classification.

RELATIVE LOCATION—A system of arranging library materials that allows new material to be intershelved at any point.

SCHEDULES—The notations of the ten main classes of the Dewey Decimal Classification system.

SCOPE NOTE—A note in DDC, *Sears,* or LCC explaining the limitations or special qualifications of a subject or notation.

SEARS—The *Sears List of Subject Headings*; used in many school and other small libraries.

SEE ALSO REFERENCE—An instruction guiding the reader from a name or term to other names or terms that are related to it.

SEE REFERENCE—An instruction guiding the reader from a name or term not used to one that is used in a catalog or reference work.

SEPARATE ENTRY—A method of noting accompanying materials in which, if an item is to circulate alone, a separate catalog description is supplied. In this case, in the strict sense of the term, the item is no longer accompanying material.

SERIAL—A publication issued in successive parts and intended to be continued indefinitely; includes such items as periodicals, newspapers, reports, and bulletins.

SHARED RESPONSIBILITY—Collaboration between persons creating a work, all of whom perform the same type of activity.

SHELF LIST—A file that is arranged in the same order as the items on the shelf.

SPECIFIC MATERIAL DESIGNATIONS—A term that indicates the specific or special class of material to which an item belongs, e.g., filmstrips, microfiche, etc.

SPECIFIC SUBJECT ENTRY—Assigning a heading that deals with the specific subject of an item, not the general class.

STANDARD SUBDIVISIONS—Table I from the DDC: notations indicating recurring forms that may be added to notations from the schedules.

SUBJECT HEADING—An access point appearing at the top of an entry, that identifies the topic of a work.

SUPPLIED TITLE—A title supplied by a cataloger to identify those items that have no title.

TABLES—A sequence of notations used in classification systems.

TAG—A device used in computerized databases that marks elements of a record to enable selective location and display. For example, one tag may be attached to each author's name, another to each title, etc.

TECHNICAL READING—An examination of certain parts of an item, especially the Chief Source of Information, as part of the cataloging process.

TERMS OF AVAILABILITY—The terms on which an item is available from the publisher, for instance, the price.

THESAURUS—An index of terms used in information retrieval, especially from a computer.

TITLE ENTRY—The catalog entry under the title of a publication.

TITLE PROPER—The chief name of an item, including an alternative title, but not other title information.

TRACINGS—Items listed on the main entry catalog record indicating other entries that have been made and filed for the same work.

TRUNCATED RECORD—A record that has been shortened.

UNIFORM HEADING—A particular heading by which a work is to be identified for cataloging purposes.

UNIFORM TITLE—A particular title for a work with several variant titles. Also a conventional collective title used for volumes containing several works.

UNION CATALOG—A catalog containing the holdings of groups of libraries or information centers.

UNIT SET—A set of catalog entries for an item identical except for the headings or access points.

UNPUBLISHED ITEMS—Locally produced material, usually accompanied by little bibliographic information to help the cataloger.

VARIABLE FIELD—In an electronic database, a field that is unrestricted as to length.

VERSO—Any left-hand page in an open book. The reverse of a RECTO.

VISIBLE FILE—A series of metal frames in which cards may be mounted with the headings showing one above another; used by libraries as a checking file for material received, and as a catalog record for periodicals.

WORD-BY-WORD FILING—Filing that observes the spaces at the end of each word. The alternative to LETTER-BY-LETTER FILING.